Skira Architecture Library

Sebastiano Brandolini

Kristian Gullichsen
Erkki Kairamo
Timo Vormala

Architecture 1969–2000

Skira

Scientific editor
Luca Molinari

Editing
Anna Albano

Layout
Paola Ranzini

Translations
Susan Wise

First published in Italy in 2000 by
Skira editore S.p.A.
Palazzo Casati Stampa
via Torino 61
20123 Milano
Italy

Printed and bound in Italy. First edition

ISBN 88-8118-655-1

Distributed in North America and Latin
America by Abbeville Publishing Group,
22 Cortlandt Street, New York,
NY 10007, USA.
Distributed elsewhere in the world by
Thames and Hudson Ltd., 181a High
Holborn, London WC1V 7QX,
United Kingdom.

Contents

Sebastiano Brandolini

A building trio

Finland's position in the geography of European architecture is special. Relegated way up there at the top, practically an appendage to Russia, Finland is proud of its history and self-sufficiency, but has always felt the need to set up lasting ties with the rest of the world; so it often welcomed, embraced, metabolised and digested conceptions and ideas born elsewhere, and then applied them better and with more care than others. It is perhaps the European country that most believed in Modernity in all its expressions and succeeded in making architecture its trademark. What Sigfried Giedion wrote about Alvar Aalto's work in *Space, Time and Architecture* (in the 1954 re-edition) shaped a way of seeing Finland for the coming years, and even today it is not easy to alter that point of view.

We often speak of the singularity of Finnish architecture, its springing from the landscape as if by magic, being made with local materials (wood, stone), being organic and blended with nature, picturesque but functional as well. It is worth quoting a paragraph from Giedion: 'Finland is wherever Aalto goes. It is the intimate source of energy ever flowing through his work. Like Spain for Picasso or Ireland for James Joyce. It is typical of the essence of contemporary art for its true exponents to draw their origin from a specific city atmosphere, and for their work not to spring from a vacuum.' Aside from establishing a connection with the geographic location, Giedion ascribes to modernity a temporal meaning as well: 'It is also typical of modernity that barriers between space and time, between various countries and between future and past are cast down; and that our time, the whole world and the whole of history merge in a bold synthesis.' Some critics have carried Giedion's thinking to extremes, to the point of seeing a connection between so-called Nordic end-of-the-century romanticism, Finnish functionalist architecture between the two world wars, the

rise of cities in the post-war period, and the last twenty-five years when countless ideas overlapped without a common theme. Today, the presumed Finland-ness has ended up by isolating Finland in the ante-chamber of the architectural debate. Finnish architecture is usually acknowledged as having the quality and capacity to combine formal conception with the exercise of doing, but not a theoretic framework offering solutions to all problems. It is precisely from that point of view that we can grasp the legacy of Alvar Aalto, whose ghost still floats today in so many works and ways of thinking, although more than twenty years have gone by since his demise in 1976. Even if for many Finnish architects Aalto is a bad ghost who makes whoever chooses him as a reference feel inadequate, we have to admit that he left a legacy of works that contain building rules that go beyond architecture: a sense of belonging, closeness, care, precision and simplicity. Aalto was able to satisfy the eye and the mind, allowing even the small man (a commonplace, but true) to have his share; he proved that it is in the small things that each of us can feel the maker of his own world, and that this leads to our physical and psychological well-being.

Kristian Gullichsen, one of the three partners of the Gullichsen Kairamo Vormala studio, grew up in a house designed (we could nearly say built, considering the degree of precision and participation with which it was thought and carried out) by Aalto, Villa Mairea. The clients, Maire and Harry, were his parents. Ever since his youth he absorbed the influx that a remarkable house communicates: distinction without ostentation, being able to get lost without ever feeling lost, the profusion of different forms that share the fluidity of space. Today at Villa Mairea Kris still knows just where to sit to have the best view, he knows how to behave formally or informally within the same space depending on the situation, he knows in which part of

Shopping centre
and Office tower,
Itäkeskus, Helsinki.
Vertical elements.

the Villa the light falls best in certain seasons or moments of the day, and he knows how to enjoy the house like a palace or a hut, as he likes. These questions of perception (which are not merely psychological) cannot be considered a prerogative of Finland, but their universality concerns architecture in its many cultural expressions, in the various points of the globe.

Today that buildings are considered consumers' goods that are not necessarily supposed to last in time but instead should be able to adjust easily and immediately to various climates and continents. But this market approach often entails dramatic approximations and shortcuts; the price of globalization, for our practical craft as architects, seems to essentially mean that. Gullichsen Kairamo Vormala's work quietly counters it all, by way of buildings that make their physicalness, visibility and concreteness, either in details or in spaces, their banner. Each design builds indissoluble bonds of solidarity between function, form and location; an essentially practical modus operandi that purposely got rid of ideologies regarding use of materials, history, style, sociology or city planning. This flexibility within the method confirms the formal multiplicity which the Modern Movement had founded and which it proved itself capable of achieving; hence the work of the studio seems to claim that architecture is a natural event, a praxis that does not require an introduction, then can speak for itself. That is why it is easy to discern big differences between each of the buildings; differences, not opposites, that show how much freedom and innocence to design and build we still can enjoy. Each design has its own story, its condition, its soul, its guardian angel.

I went to see most of the buildings with Kristian Gullichsen. Each one was introduced to me as though it were a friend with whom he had shared an adventure, like a place laden with memories and expectancies. Each space has its own precise physiognomy pulsing with energy, thought out in the studio or on site and perfectly suited to the use made of it. Each design has its legacy of anecdotes that make you smile, because they tell the truth about architecture and the life that goes on in its orbit. About Villa Haltia at Kangasala, built recently in the agricultural region in the southwest of the country,

Gullichsen tells that the client, a surgeon, had asked for a Tuscan villa, but that it had turned out looking like a Lombard house, and fortunately the client liked it that way. In that laconic humour we can see a close connection with Aalto, although it may simply mean a high degree of identification between the maker and the work, i.e., between the architect and his design. Gullichsen believes that one of the strengths of architecture is to improve the spirit of life and the quality of our relationship with the world.

Such optimism, we might say, is a fundamental aspect of Gullichsen Kairamo Vormala's work. Within the studio each of the three partners (Kairamo died in 1994) followed (without becoming specialised) his own family of buildings, which in the course of years became more and more recognisable in their characteristics: Gullichsen the public buildings, Kairamo the industrial and commercial ones, Vormala the residential sector. What those three directions of research shared was the conviction that they should follow at any cost the linear evolution of the rational, poetic principles of the Modern Movement: in Finland, unlike other European countries, there seems to be a substantial agreement about what that term means, and how it originated in the early twenties and developed onwards; far from being ambiguous, the Modern Movement is still a compass useful today for various vessels that otherwise might well go adrift. For our three architects modernity possesses resources for further formal articulations: in the inner organisation of spaces, in the relationship with the city and the landscape, in the choice of materials, in the typological evolution and the collective image buildings communicate. Their designs cannot be classified by styles, they neither celebrate the past nor anticipate the future. They are rooted in the *hic et nunc*, entrenched in the location and the moment in which they were built.

A good example is the Varkaus Power station, which Erkki Kairamo designed in 1990, at a time when the hi-tech style was widely successful and becoming less and less industrial and formally more and more convoluted (we need only think of the works by Rogers or Grimshaw). This building, compact and quite large despite appearances, uses technology to purposes that are the opposite of hi-tech, meaning to be simplified and reduced to its lowest terms; the elevations do not celebrate the impermanence of the assembling, but emphasise the central role of industry and paper in city life. Nothing is left to chance; the pure volumes of the power station were designed in all their aspects while considering everything from the observer's point of view: distance, light, shadows, skyline. The details are full of vibrations since they perform several tasks at once, sharing in the composition on several scales; they are sensuous and never redundant, dry, necessary and functional. Kairamo plays cleverly with dimensional scales, always setting up a first and a second plane: a first element that serves as a gauge to give us the dimension (for instance an emergency stairway), and another element whose size is not measurable and that serves as background. At the same time Kairamo appears to use architecture as if it were a thermometer, staging playfulness with temperatures: the hot energy produced by the power plant blends with the cold, quiet and carefully-dosed energy of metal, the material it is made of. This design contains a great many 'small things' that balance each other in the general design, producing both variety and regularity. Hence even the energy industry becomes domestica-

ted, yet without losing its characteristics which are the grandeur and purity of its forms, not so far removed from those of American grain silos that Gropius, Le Corbusier and Mendelsohn had celebrated in their time, and later Banham had evoked.

Gullichsen Kairamo Vormala's devotion to small things goes well beyond the skilful execution of constructive details. Small things are a sentimental added value which the project offers to whoever lives in it or examines it with an attentive eye. Small things stress that slight difference whereby simplicity becomes poetry. Other examples: the bench carved out of the wall right by the entrance door where you can wait or sit to catch a ray of sun (Olympos Urban villas, Myllitie, Helsinki), the railing which, used to fence the parking lot, tells the story of the place (Civic center, Pieksämäki), the building used as a training gym for firemen (Fire station, Espoo). These episodes, subtle and anything but random, form a second level of interpretation of the building in respect to its overall design; they express a pleasure producing a slow, lasting flavour that the image does not wear out, and is all the deeper the more casual was our discovery. They are epi-

Civic centre Poleeni,
Pieksämäki.
Interior view.

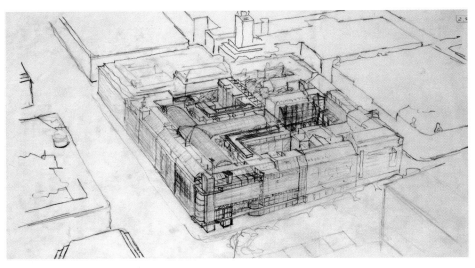

sodes that leave traces in our memory, to then resurface in association with something else, launching a chain of thoughts and reflections of which architecture is one of the links. All our senses are involved in this play of references and allusions.

The Fire station at Espoo (1991) contains a whole bunch of surprises; here Kairamo turned each of the client's functional requirements into an architectural figure, using it playfully, and transfiguring it with authentic self-irony and thorough seriousness. Just imagine a three-dimensional gym of outside walls all set up for firemen's practice, and which was a training ground for the architect as well; here an emergency can actually be staged, and the firemen can practice live every hurdle and every danger, and experience the dizziness and fears of their profession. It does not look like those synthetic rock walls made in countless city gyms; here nothing is fake or simulated, everything is true and useful. To understand the position of every hook, platform or structural element it would be a good idea to identify with the users and be firemen; but architects too can have fun here, getting lost in the ingeniousness of the details where you can find structural pieces, decorative pieces and pieces for practice, maybe even discovering which of these pieces can do more than one thing at a time. Refined metal carpentry works, the frames that form this building look from some angles like chisel works because of the way they cut out bits of sky and how out of

nothing the structure becomes a silhouette. The frames, by giving form to the gym-skin of the building, delineate real three-dimensional volumes, hence communicating a sense of fulness; they are not scaffolds made to be taken apart.

As a result, even the loud-speakers, bicycles and fire-trucks placed around the Fire station belong to the composition, and look carefully designed. The tower, that aims at being like a lighthouse visible from afar, is in fact even more precious when seen from close up. Sensuous in its constructive coldness, possibly inspired by the WChUTEMAS sculpture exercises of the early 1920s, the tower is a decorative object as well, that could be miniaturised and provide tactile delight to our hands. And even if it is decoration, Erkki Kairamo's authentically personal research never gives an impression of excess or waste, but aims at dignifying *utilitas* so as to become an architectural form. Several parts of the architectural composition, which is in part reminiscent of embroidery, are red; and while this colour is decorative, it also plays the role of a signal.

Perhaps in the contemporary world of globalization we can no longer believe in the authenticity of a region or a cultural context: maybe the only authenticity left is the one embodied in the quality of the idea, in the integrity of the reasoning, and in the level of depth the building achieves. The idea of context Gullichsen Kairamo Vormala promote is not the traditional one that assumes sharing well-defined formal rules. Their idea is free of ties and based on a vague but tangible concept of appropriateness to the location. 'Architecture should be like a shoe', Gullichsen says, 'something precise, close-fitting, right for this or that specific ground, guaranteeing the right amount of perspiration and fashioned around its own inner functions; it should be closely connected both with the weather and with time.' Gullichsen firmly believes in the naturalness of architecture and that it is not a place of conflict but of reconciliation. A building that provides a good description of the advantages of this approach is the extension of the Stockmann Department store in downtown Helsinki, where the industrial soul and that of civil representation of architecture coincide and recompose the ill-assorted parts of a city block.

It is the most urban of all the works the studio has executed, a sort of blow-up of Pierre Chareau's 1933 Maison de Verre, but located on the corner of a block instead of overlooking an inner courtyard. Viewed formally, this unobtrusive architecture is connected with its surroundings yet is full of avant-garde rashness; it is practically all skin (surface), and that skin shows the essence of the commercial function behind it. The Stockmann extension connects an imposing building by Sigurd Frosterus — bricks, pillars and vertical windows — and the small Argos château — all towers and frills. On Keskuskatu, the main street the building looks onto, several outstanding buildings of the history of Finnish architecture are lined up; an Eliel Saarinen building and two by Alvar Aalto set the standard. The facades, harmonised by their plain rhythms and the tactile organisation of their details, are nonetheless different: a 'romanesque' front for Saarinen, a 'classicist' one for Frosterus, modern for Aalto; the weak northern light carves out their shadows, while the long twilight hours highlight the window frames. Compared to these noble street companions, the new Stockmann has a different surface; if in the other buildings the opaque facades are barely altered by the passing of the hours of the day and the seasons, here the reinforced concrete and glass tiles surface changes constantly: it is a source of light during the night time and the winter months; and a reflecting but opaque wall during the daytime and the summer months. The phenomenology of the

building alternates between the 'clearly visible' of a source of light, and the 'nearly invisible' of an elegant glass building. More a response to the weather conditions than to the urban context, the new Stockmann keeps up an open, unpredictable, yet dialectic dialogue with its location. A statement on how to intervene in the context, the Keskuskatu facade alters the meaning of several elements taken from Frosterus' next-door building: some horizontal alignments are extended, the brick dormer-windows become small glassed-in terraces, a row of small vertical windows are turned into modern ribbon windows. Around the corner, on Pohjoisesplanadi, a composition with lots of exceptions helps it cohabit with the Argos building: a jutting hanging garden, a vertical blade, a half-moon balcony, a mast. All this without radical changes in the materials.

Over the past twenty years, in big and small European cities alike, we have seen the improvement of design instruments for intervening wisely in historic city centres. We have learned how to adjust our ideas when working for restoration, rehabilitation or alteration, and we know how to tear down and rebuild without causing irreparable damage to the legacy of the past. From that point of view, the Stockmann extension is the result of a long discussion carried out since the 1960s on the subject of historic centres. But in the meantime we have also grown over-addicted to historic centres; so that many architects, even when building in outlying suburbs, or in less dense conditions than city centres, still think and design as if they were in a stratified, crowded fabric, or as if the 'historic centre effect' were the objective to be achieved. As a matter of fact it is not exceptional, in Finland and elsewhere, to find in the suburbs buildings that strive to mean more than they can, and by doing so they do not preserve and even less enhance the intrinsic qualities of the diffused city. That problem is shared by many countries, pointing to the profound split between the figures of the city planner and the architect: each one seems to have his own idea of the city, which the other does not share in theory nor support in practice.

Gullichsen Kairamo Vormala have the merit of having worked on typical suburban buildings without wanting to upset their constitutive rules, confirming them instead, and erecting buildings offering these locations a lasting physical quality. A number of collecti-

Villa Haltia, Kangasala.
Windows seen
from without and within.

ve buildings they designed belong to areas of city expansion: churches, civic centres, shopping centres and public services, as well as residential quarters, of course. None of these buildings aim at emulating the historical functions of city centres; instead, each one is exemplary by the opposite: on the one hand it realistically identifies with the indifferent sprawling of the contemporary Finnish city, and on the other it shapes the needs and aspirations of whoever lives, works and uses his car to move about there.

At Pieksämäki, in central Finland, Gullichsen Karamo Vormala have built a Civic centre (completed in 1989) that is an example of the simplicity on which suburban life could be based. It is a deep building, a couple of storeys high, with two long facades, one facing the street and the other a public park, each one marked by a series of small significant events: a portal, a hanging garden, a cut, a fold, a fireplace room, a copper canopy, a corner tower, a smokestack. For the designers these elements are a tribute to the past and to friends: the Venetian chimney-pot, the Michelangelo portal, the hearth of old country houses, the Aalto-style canopy, the medieval tower; far from being mere quotations, each one of them is an actor requested to improvise a part. Silvia Milesi nicely described the atmosphere of this nearly primordial place: 'Here nature has not undergone major interventions, except the ones undertaken to leave room for modest, quiet homes ... Every gesture performed is emphasised by the absence of strong signs nearby ... This condition asks architecture for intrinsic spatial qualities, rather than capacities to alter the context, and a sound functionality that simply improves life.' And then, referring to the design background: 'The local community turned the need to represent the city's social life into a precise architectural demand, mediating between Finnish architectural culture and local popular decision-making, inexperienced and malleable, hesitant and receptive, vague yet pragmatic.' The Civic centre not only organised the many-sided program, but even enhanced it; the town library, the cafeteria with its combined spaces, the gallery and the theatre are all linked to one another, forming a single large public space where more than one function overlap and follow hard on each other. At times you might worry about an excess of casualness in the layout of these spaces, despite the overall sense of the

design. But that 'disorder' was probably meant from the first sketches, insofar as it succeeds in creating the very sense of hierarchy and uncertainty that is so lacking in the existing Pieksämäki.

The building, about one hundred meters long and yet flexible enough to curve like an arch alongside the park, offers a catalogue of borderline situations that expand our visual perception enabling us to range through spheres belonging to the imagination: 'the extremely beautiful emotion of feeling oneself "facing" the world and at the same time "reassured" by the privilege of occupying a front-row position', as Silvia Milesi writes. The sequence of the entrance includes a huge portal (clearly visible from afar), a small courtyard (where the ceremony of arrival takes place, with the features of a cour d'honneur), a high hall (where the two inner stairways merge) and, across from it, a tiny fireplace room (where you can dry off in case it is snowing). At one end of the building there is the tower room, where children can read while imagining a medieval atmosphere, and whence they can also see without being seen. There is nothing fake or pretended in the use of these flashes addressed to the past and to our subconscious, but instead the conviction that their disappearance in the today's world is unjustified and implies an inner deprivation of ourselves. Outside, towards the garden, there is a low wall made of the stones used by farmers to mark property limits, while alongside the street a long bench is in fact a raised railroad rail, recalling the important railway connection role Pieksämäki and its 15,000 inhabitants played in the history of Finland. Each architectural choice has several purposes at once, and works on different epistemological levels.

If the huge order of the windows makes the Pieksämäki Civic centre recognisable as a public building, the glass facades do the same for the Shopping centre and Tower of Itäkeskus, a satellite city east of Helsinki, built in 1987. Two remarkably large volumes, one horizontal and the other vertical, oppose each other balancing their dynamic thrust; hence the composition can be seen from the nearby freeway (with the fast flow of cars) as well as from the surrounding lower residential districts for which the tower is like an orientation compass. A number of details of the design reveal the fondness Erkki Kairamo felt for the compositional mechanisms of

Malmi Church, Helsinki.
Counterpoise of brick
and glass forms.

Soviet constructivism, even if here they undergo a metamorphosis, losing their controversial vein and putting on instead gentle, tactile clothing, not in the least aggressive. Fashioning glass and metal so as to communicate sensuality is by no means simple, especially when the scale of the design is large and the budget not particularly generous.

The elements forming the Shopping centre spring from the same building system, creating a plentiful abacus of details and solutions; their repetition and careful placing on the buildings (on the corner, in the middle, isolated, high up, down low, jutting outwards and inwards) produce a variety whose rules are always clearly legible. Strolling on the outer street that serves as the main entrance (in summer occupied by tables and benches, marked by vertical shop signs), we are delighted at how this architecture is able to produce real life and activities, not pretences. It reminds us of a 1924 article by Alvar Aalto, written after his honeymoon with Aino in Italy, where he complained about there not being any markets in Finland; 'Kauppatori, kauppahalli, kauppakuia' ('Piazza, market, bazar') describes the market as the synthesis of urban life and European piazzas, and insists that in Jyväkylä it should be located, with its porticoes, in an outstanding place,

meaning next to the church.

It is nice to imagine that at Itäkeskus Kairamo, instead of a shopping centre, wanted a market; that is the first impression. The fact that some stores can be reached from outside and others from inside was undoubtedly a determining choice, because it doubled the frontage, created a relationship with the surroundings and with the traffic flow, producing a combined situation including an outside and an inside. The long inside gallery on several levels has a glass shed roof, that recalls a neighbourhood market before the days of shopping centres. We sense that a good part of the public is here to be among other people as well as to shop, and that the visual pressures connected with shopping are (thanks to the architecture) less pressing than in other like structures; it's as though the shop-keepers had carved out their own sales space, seeking a kind of intimacy with the buyer. Thus the commercial program was interpreted by the architects in a social key as well, so that today the building conveys energy to the city and a positive approach to suburban life.

The plan for Itäkeskus includes, aside from the buildings of the Shopping centre spread out horizontally, a 16 story tower with an outer stairway 82 metres high, and which

Lyökkiniemi
Semi-detached houses
in Westend, Espoo.
Cut-away perspective
sketch and metal
carpentry detail.

is taller than the roof, ending in a trellis. The architectural purpose was to design a narrow, soaring building, with a clearly legible verticality; to limit the encumbrance of the central core and animate the facades, the vertical elements of the services were placed on the outside. Actually the tower looks squat in its overall proportions, but the outer stairway, especially when seen from below during the twilight hours, is like a soaring burst of flame. The outer surfaces of the square plan offer a rich three-dimensional articulation: two of the four corners have the motif of square balconies, the two others triangular balconies; they look like they are hanging onto the glass walls, and since the identical ones are at opposite corners you never see them at the same time. The wall part of each facade, projecting slightly beyond the corner balconies, contains ribbon windows and is different on every side, because of the service columns and the tall stairway. The roof is a landscape describing the up-and-down motion of the various forms and materials: antennas, walkways, stairways, frames. Far from being pure and abstract, the tower lets itself be contaminated by the elements forming it, and by doing so describes its own liveability; the architectural play takes place on the uncertain borderline between order and disorder. On the ground level there is no respect zone nor a real entrance hall; the latter is replaced by a double-height space (with a nearly homey atmosphere) containing a cafeteria open to the public. Both in the shopping centre and in the tower, Kairamo used a Cartesian matrix in which the horizontal and vertical elements are equal, in thickness, design and tectonic weight. The identity of this work, anything but commercial, can be referred to a flexible building matrix devoid of symbolic meanings. The frame, with its many variations, is the tool shaping Itäkeskus, opening and closing our views and unfolding in various directions.

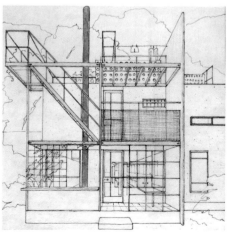

When the three partners Kristian Gullichsen, Erkki Kairamo and Timo Vormala formed the studio, their interest in the frame, and its formal ambiguities and potentials, was probably what drew them together on the grounds of reciprocal interest. In 1973 Gullichsen had worked with Juhani Pallasmaa on the pre-fabrication system called 'Moduli', Kairamo had already designed and built several small residential quarters based on the notion of growth, whereas Vormala, a few years younger, had already shown his interest in housing as the main connective fabric of the city. Vormala's role made it possible for two such different and potentially conflicting designers as Gullichsen and Kairamo to harmoniously coexist; over the years, he proved that it is possible to build a good deal of projects of high quality without necessarily each time needing to be original, but just by way of slight transpositions and local inventions. The three partners made abundant use of the tools of continuity, simplicity and sound construction, rather than of styles.

The promotional folder described 'Moduli' as 'a true construction game'; and we might add that Moduli was a hybrid between Lego (based on blocks) and Meccano (based on the structure). Its main trait was to guarantee, aside from a constructive flexibility, a perceptive flexibility as well. Each element functioned either as structural component (vertical, horizontal, furnishing) or as a modulator: able to screen and calibrate views, light, transparency and texture. Each client could choose the design and compose the parts of his house; depending on the configuration the design could be introverted or extroverted; you could include windows or absorb small inner courtyards, and choose whether or not to keep visible the pillars and bearing beams; the structure rested on a wooden platform raised above the ground. It was undeniably a natural prefabrication, since it was entirely made of wood.

The photographs show Moduli in the midst of the woods; the tree trunks blend and merge with its vertical structure, while the horizontality of floor and ceiling contrasts with the uneven, slightly slanting ground; it is typical Finnish terrain formed by large surfaces of rock marked by glaciers, which depending on the season are covered with moss and lichen, or covered over with light underbrush. Thanks to the precision of its orthogonal design, Moduli is a non-temporary structure made to age; the frames placed alongside one another stand for a simple lifestyle without unnecessary luxuries, combining the adventure of camping out with the comforts of home.

The materials differ but the substance is the same, in the holiday home Gullichsen designed for himself at Grasse, in the south of France, in that gentle Mediterranean climate

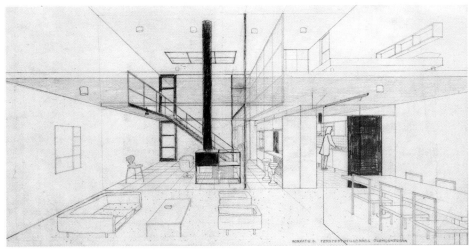

Liinasaarenkatu Terraced houses, Espoo. Perspective sketch.

which so influenced modern architecture and Aalto. Like Moduli, the Petite Maison of 1972 is an exercise in camouflage, which does not attempt to disappear entirely but to dissolve in a play of dual identities, hiding so as to then intentionally be found. The location is the steep terraces cultivated with olive groves on the Côte d'Azur; the height of the house corresponds to the retaining walls, the rooms being sheltered underground with ample views onto the landscape. Each room (loggia, kitchen, living room, two bedrooms, facilities with a sauna) is evenly spaced out, and features on the facade a double fenestration including a French window and sliding shutters, that can be viewed as a piece of Moduli. When the shutters are closed the stone walls make the house disappear in the landscape, whereas with the shutters open the walls become pillars; hence with the slightest effort, the house from being a block becomes a stone frame; and that is another variation of its dual identity, balanced between closed and open onto the surrounding nature.

The works Erkki Kairamo executes in the early 1970s can be considered analogous to those of Kristian Gullichsen at the same period. All too often critics have insisted on the fact that Kairamo, genuinely in love with the light forms of the 1930s, had then pursued that line of enquiry nearly regardless of what had happened or was happening meanwhile. Actually Kairamo, in spite of using original elements of the functionalism and constructivism of those years, always brought them up to date (without dwelling

on nostalgia), exploring in charcoal sketches a new image that would be optimistic and appropriate for the future: adding elements, overlaying various materials, using metal frames and parts, creating a range of intermediary spaces between inside and outside, combining the parts so as to create places with a marked collective significance. For about twenty years Espoo, a mainly residential district about twenty kilometres west of Helsinki, was Kairamo's experimental laboratory; he measured himself here with various housing projects, each one with its own density and configuration: Hannika Houses at Suomenoja in 1970, Linasaarentie Multifamily house in 1971, Liinasaarenkuja Semidetached houses in 1980, Hiiralankaari Apartment block in 1983, and Lyökkiniemi Semi-detached houses in 1990.

Hannika Houses are homes built with a combined metal and wood frame and mortar infills. Linear and light, they take advantage of their length and the slope of the land to have a single story on the back (where you approach and park your car) and two on the front (where a two-level loggia offers views on the landscape of land and water). The flat roof is brought to life by two out of scale but typically domestic elements: a metal railing going around the loggia and the living-room on two levels, and a cylindrical chimney rising way above the profile of the roof. The essence of the design lies in the calibrated overlapping of inside and outside; it is a three-dimensional overlapping visible on each of the six sides of the house's parallelepiped: on four

facades, on the roof overlooking the sky, and also on the ground floor that addresses the topography of the land. The building is like a palafitte (pile-dwelling), visually connected with the ground only at entrance level, with a small courtyard built upon a stone ballast.

In his contemporary design of the Linasaarentie Multi-family house in 1971 Kairamo uses the same repertory of forms, although this time dealing with a low-cost building in a far from scenic landscape. Here the compositional method is more complicated than in the Hannika houses, blending technical and aesthetic aspects: around a core of pre-fabricated panels forming the bearing structure, structurally independent elements are fixed, giving the ensemble a vibrant image, interrupting the rhythm of the structure and creating a new visual order. To differentiate the metal and wood parts, the balconies, rails, fences, infills and inner elements, bright but not primary colours were widely used; the resulting effect is Spartan and typical of an architecture easy to build, to live in and to upkeep. The house, although based on a technical-constructive idea, does not show its muscles or its mechanisms; so that Kairamo, to praise its innocent lightness, playfully compares it to a 'house of cards'.

In the following years, Kairamo pursues his enquiry addressing a new formal definition of housing; actually he tempers the houses with various elements external to the structure but necessary to their functions and to the narrative the design is supposed to achieve, thereby putting into practice the function-fiction binary couple Gullichsen talks about; that couple contains the two opposites imposed on architecture, and which architecture tries to make coincide. In the Low-density quarter of Liinasaarenkuja in 1980, Kairamo proves that the bearing part and the non-bearing part of a house are equipollent and can balance each other: the terraces, the stairways, the frames and garden accessories become the essence of the habitation itself. Later in the Hiiralankaari Apartment block in 1983 he shows how the frame of the mortar structure can present values of domesticity and extend in the design the form of the metal carpentry loggias and rails. The facades of this building (that combines elements of a slab block and of row housing) are crystalline and produce a sense of rational order without underestimating the particular details of each unit: a positive approach to housing that is precious also in reference to the historical period in which it was carried out. The early 1980s, it is

worthwhile recalling, were ruled by extremes: rationalism obsessed by the modularity of geometry clashed with post-modernism blinded by the idioms of history, while both styles had entirely given up the dialectic research the modern movement had encouraged.

Kairamo's housing works and Gullichsen's Moduli appear to be drawn true to scale. I am not only referring to the simple accuracy with which the details were thought and carried out, but especially to a question of perception, meaning the fact that, when we draw near, the buildings from visual become tactile, and naturally combine the scale of the architecture with the scale of man, the eye and the hand. Bringing together construction and perception demands a special feeling for and a fond interest in ordinary things and the practice of the profession. Each architectural element serves several purposes at once and has a number of functions; we might say it is multi-purpose. To understand the building you have to go beyond observation and identify with its use, since only by using it can you fully possess it. Our architects seem to be aware of the fact that the building will have a life that goes on after being conceived and built; the architectural language and forms chosen contain *in nuce* a series of suggestions about how the project will be altered and age over the years; a sort of veiled encouragement to 'do it yourself', naturally within architectural rules shared by all.

Near the centre of Helsinki, the Näkinpuisto Housing block (1989) states both a civil monumentality and a typically Nordic modesty; Gullichsen Kairamo Vormala were aware that only by calibrating finishings, facades, interior spaces, proportions, materials and views could they generate an architecture detached from the nineteenth-century fabric of the area, and which at the same time would be of quality and normality, even if that might seem a contradiction. The project is located in a highly-populated district not far from the harbour, which influenced the option of a building closed on a courtyard with the outer facades faced in brick, and a clear contrast between interior and exterior. Let us take a look at the outer perimeter: the symmetry of the various entrances suits the slightly sloping ground, the materials are arranged so as to create the illusion of a single building rather than a lot of houses bunched next to one another; the windows are grouped in correspondence with the corners so as to reduce the specific weight of the brick facades, the bottoms of the lifts look like large chimneys, while the steep slopes of the roofs can only be seen from a certain distance. On the contrary, on the inner courtyard, the main colours of the facades are white and pale blue so as to increase the light, with only part of the base in brick; here the balconies are cement and glass tiles whereas the penthouses of the top stories are small glassed-in pavilions with an industrial flavour. The garden — which is a real garden — is large enough to contain its own vegetation and the communal life of the block.

At Näkinpuisto, like in so many of the studio's housing projects in recent years (for instance, the Foka and Spinnu Projects in Helsinki), a great deal of care was given to the perimeter of the building, which by analogy reminds us of the frame of a painting. The perimeter, as a line, marks the zones of shadow and light, establishes the boundary

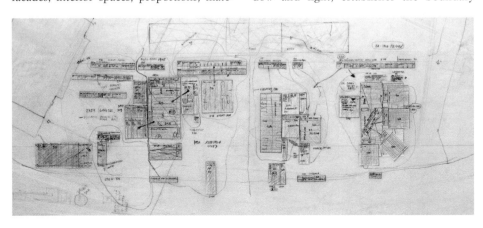

Biomedicum Centre,
Helsinki. Interior and
exterior perspectives.

between what the public sees and what the private uses, and evidences objects having different weights and materials, like walls, windows, balconies, roofs, entrances. Vormala is responsible for most of the studio's housing production; he has the merit of believing that housing can and must play a cardinal role in our cities and of having acknowledged its visibility. Even in Finland, housing construction is afflicted with rules and standards that reduce every idea to the norm, whether it be buildings or developments of high or low density. Vormala knows how to add a dose of spirit to the predictability of that typology, treating it as if it were naturally open to innovation, without trying to be either original at any cost or redundant.

We can also find principles of normality, with a patina of refinement, in the Olympos Urban villas Kristian Gullichsen designed and completed in 1995. They occupy a special panoramic position overlooking the passenger terminal of the Helsinki port. The city fabric here is made up of small and medium-sized buildings (there are several official buildings, embassies, companies), all at a proper distance one from another, surrounded by greenery and owing nothing to the topography of the landscape. Ever since the competition project Gullichsen confronted the theme with aggressively disregarding the slightest hint of shyness towards the city and seeking direct contact with its natural forms, clearly visible from here. To achieve this aim, he used two images dear to modernists: that of the village perched on the crown of a hill (which obsessed Aalto for years — see for instance Villa Mairea and the Säynätsalo Town Hall), and that of the ship broken down to its various parts (a theme that had intrigued Kairamo too, see the Lyökkiniemi Semi-detached houses of 1990).

On the new Mount Olympus, the two 'urban villas' are nearly identical, but they are mirrored and slightly offset on the bisector axis placed at a 45° angle to the plan of the composition. Placing ourselves on that axis, we can observe the same facade twice, and recognise elements of continuity even in the variety of the design. Thanks to this stratagem, the two villas seem to be interlocked, like two pieces of a jigsaw puzzle about to be joined. In the space between the two pieces lies the entrance courtyard formed by a sequence of forms jutting in and out made in

the thickness of the facades; on the opposite side, towards the harbour, the facades stretch, improving the views and sun exposure. Gullichsen's imagination includes ample hanging gardens on the roof that emphasise Helsinki's assumed Mediterranean character, and down below robust mortar footings mediate with the geology of the land. Of course a more prosaic imagination is present as well: small stone walls, sand-boxes for children, pebble sidewalks, wooden pergolas, roof terraces for hanging out laundry. That is precisely, you might say, the architect's task, torn between two forces to be combined: private experimentation and public responsibility. When the scale of residential projects is conspicuous, it becomes increasingly difficult to control its domesticity. On one hand repetition is welcome on a logical level, on the other it can become an obstacle on a perception one. It is the chief problem Timo Vormala encountered in designing the Meritähti Apartments and the Kesäkatu Apartment blocks, both in the western suburbs of Helsinki. Their scale is nevertheless far from suburban. Glazed corner and projected balconies are stacked one over the other, producing a kind of Atelier Ozenfant (Le Corbusier, 1923) multiplication effect; the chimney flues are so evident that one wonders whether they play a structural role as well; the skyline and the base are properly modulated. As one meanders along or through the composite buildings forming the blocks, one enjoys three-dimensional views and one sees the same thing more than once and from more than one angle. This effects a sense of security and homeliness, reinforced by the natural contexts (sea and woods) surrounding the buildings.

In examining two projects by Gullichsen's hand presently under construction, you can recognise a compositional method (that consists in adding on rather than subtracting) that hovers on the brink of the picturesque. Both are outside Finland: the Finnish Embassy in Stockholm in Sweden and the Library of the University of Lleida in Spain. The model pictures of the two projects look like they suffer from an excess of architectural elements, too crowded together. But it is probably too early to judge, since the construction just started; only when finished and inhabited can buildings be fully appraised.

At Stockholm, the main facade of the Embassy is to be a large wall devoted to the phenomenology of architecture; it will feature a catalogue of windows, an uneven skyline formed by chimneys and hanging gardens, various materials and an ambiguous hierarchy that leaves you wondering where representation begins and domesticity ends. The small inner courtyard will have large windows (providing light in winter) and a lot of niches and projections; these will cut out an uneven space controlled by the triangulation contained between the entrance portico, the entrance to the Embassy and a masonry cylindrical tower belonging to the Consulate.

The Library of Lleida forms the corner of a large block inside the university campus. The outer facades on the street look north, those on the courtyard south; the courtyard contains an asymmetrical drum volume to be used as a congress hall. The building plays on the theme and degrees of transparency; the facades are mostly blind (with few windows — high and narrow, round, with balcony, arched — that give a nearly vernacular touch to the ensemble), alternating with facades that look like mega-screens, as if they were huge Venetian blinds. The interior two-level volumes give the illusion of a space whose luminosity is adjustable and can thus interact with the outside in different ways depending on the season. About 15 metres high, the corner portico that serves as entrance-gallery and which a flight of stairs then connects with the inner courtyard, does indeed state its public vocation, and it does so with rhetoric and purposely out of scale. The four ground floor rooms that form the south-east head withdraw gradually creating a stepped front; that is an option which springs from a desire for form and has little to do with a true sense of necessity.

At Stockholm as at Lleida, images and volumes are carefully designed. The two planimetric compositions — both with courtyards — are lively, but to please they maybe hide their logical and structural matrix. That is the risk you take when working under the influence of images.

Quite a few of the Gullichsen Kairamo Vormala studio's design options are based on the imaginary. Still today, talking about images, the imaginary and imagination in architecture is taboo: an issue you cannot approach, as if it were unsound ground or a rock wall without holds. Many feel that having 'imagination' means having 'superficial ideas'. And yet, in front of the blank sheet of paper or the

monitor of a computer, the game many architects have to play has precisely to do with their capacity to produce 'good images'. The ones springing today from Kristian Gullichsen and Timo Vormala's four hands verge on the normality common sense demands, but are then slightly displaced from the median line of things, and this produces a sense of being lost that delights us with a sense of natural surprise; and all this with a gentleness that does not seek to astonish or shock us.

If Sigfried Giedion spoke of the spatio-temporal correspondence between Aalto and the Finnish landscape, today the figures produced by Gullichsen and Vormala would seem to refer to a broader temporal field and a wider geographic area. Their architecture is international because it is able to draw ideas from different moments of history and various points of geography, obviously not because of ambitions of conquest beyond the borders of Finland; the range of its interests belongs to the framework of the figuration and the abstraction of modernity, and over the years has assimilated both the techniques of building and the expressiveness of the visual arts. For Gullichsen modernity has a slightly nostalgic flavour, nearly antique, that nonetheless goes beyond fashions: 'Modern architecture invented new forms by using old technologies, whereas post-modern architecture uses old forms inventing new technologies'. That is an idea of modernity that is broad, hybrid, rich and complex, but always selective and distilled.

It is a modernity that has gotten rid of the theories that up to the sixties sought a revolution in lifestyles compared to the past; a modernity based on the qualities of understatement. An aspect we see for instance in the parish centre in Kauniainen (1978–1983), a quiet residential suburb west of Helsinki. Although it is a prayer centre, here religion is not in the least monumentalized, but merely described. If we compare this project with the imaginative Catholic churches thronging Italian, French or Spanish suburbs (but also the Anglican churches recently built in Finland, for instance Juha Leiviskä's Männistö Parish church and Centre at Kuopio), its frugality leaps to the eye, seeming to wish to communicate to people the pastoral vocation of the Church. The Centre features a series of striking aspects (a modern *via crucis*?), each one inspiring the act of prayer: a large blind brick wall, a passage with an arched pergola,

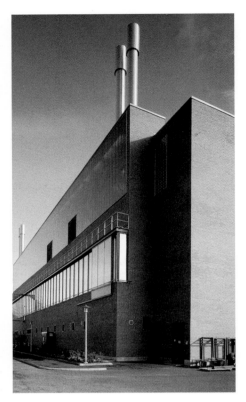

On this page and
the following page:
VTT, Micro
Electronics Center,
Espoo, Otaniemi.
Exterior views and
first floor plan.

a long lateral stairway, an inner courtyard that also serves as a cloister. Each of these architectural moments reminds us of a religious event, and prepares our spirit for an inner peace; we stand in front of the brick wall and contemplate the climbing plants that find their way on a wooden frame creating a shifting play of shadows, or we pause in the courtyard and peer into the inner space of the church, or else we stroll under the pergola as if it were a small outdoor nave. It is a many-sided view of religion: we repeatedly re-enter the same sacred space, described to us each time with different instruments.

Geometric forms — positive and negative — form a sequence of visual points of view and a sense of ritual; on the main facade niches and protuberances mark the ascension, as we walk past a triangular skylight that carves out the light to illuminate the sacristy below. The skyline is made up of triangular and pyramidal skylights that light up the inside of the church, and by the bell tower located in the courtyard and that serves as barycentre of the ensemble. The church space is a slightly trapezoidal space, with the altar placed laterally to the entrance; its position is indicated by an equilateral triangle of natural light cut out in the wooden ceiling, and by a slant of light on the facade; here the tools of minimalism are used to create a complex, layered composition. In front of the altar, a colonnade composes a low portico: it reminds us that we are below ground level. The zenithal light falls illuminating the splayed thickness of three windows, creating the effect of glowing, perfectly focused pictures.

Light is an element of design too in the recently-built colombarium located beneath the outer side of the courtyard. Here it falls in rays from seven deep wells backed against the outer facade, featuring just a few windows to mark the physical separation from the surroundings. On the other hand, the outer paving goes all the way into the bowels of the colombarium, because rites and processions should belong to the public sphere of urban life (even if it is suburban). To the two sets of stairs placed next to the large blind wall (the first aligned with the portico of the courtyard and the second climbing along the side of the building) is thus added a third passage, chtonian, wandering into the ground.

It would be difficult, and maybe futile too, to put the works of the Gullichsen Kairamo Vormala studio in a time sequence;

together they do not form a concatenation; instead they share the fact that 'the only theory possible today is the non-theory', as Gullichsen claims. Today many architects are contaminated by haste, which determines their technical and aesthetic choices; many of them would like to hurry up and address history, so they can speed up the pace and sacrifice quality to get there first. Such has never been the ambition of our Finnish architects, who never got there first, never invented a style, nor promised miracles nor promoted their own image with other means than their works. Their ideas unfolded gradually in the buildings they built, which seem to endeavour to oppose the world's apparent speed and slow down the pace of events; there is nothing old-fashioned about all this, but there is the belief that architecture cannot be subjected to forcing, and that haste cannot replace the natural flow of time.

Gullichsen uses an amusing anecdote to explain architecture: 'Architecture is like an elephant: strong and sturdy, nimble but unable to suddenly change directions. So it is not like a butterfly. Elephants and architecture are intelligent, but they can learn only a few things; they live for many years, and both have an exceptional memory. Not like butterflies that, living just a day, do not need memory. Since they are faithful and friendly to us, elephants and architecture should be treated with care and respect.'

Many architects do not see the difference between the passing of time and history. Indeed, many of them (with a large dose of presumption) think they can decide whether or not to be protagonists believing that architecture can undergo constant revolutions and repeatedly change directions like a butterfly. So their concern about history and the place they will occupy in history often substitutes the true profession, our craft of making buildings with care. With their projects Gullichsen Kairamo Vormala have given us a concrete interpretation of the slow unfolding of time; they have decided not to cut the umbilical cord with modernity, but instead to reinforce their ties with 'the handsome examples of our century' which they have chosen among their memories. They have represented the passing of time in the physicalness of the buildings; they have designed passages that cover a precise distance, placed clearly visible entrance doors, gauged the shadows of the different hours of the day,

carved the light with neat cuts or with chiaroscuro effects according to the function, thus personifying the places where the buildings stand.

Whether they be residential, industrial or institutional buildings, isolated or in urban contexts, they constantly endeavour to design places of quality, discreet enough to not cast disparaging light on their surroundings. For them, creating a place means thinking without rhetorics about a series of gestures: departing, seeking, perhaps pausing and observing the shifting light, arriving at the door, entering, putting down your umbrella, looking back at where you arrived from, sitting down. That sequence includes a series of perceptions, from light to materials, from slope to views, from shapes to sounds.

The places designed by Gullichsen Kairamo Vormala are sturdy. In the thickness of the walls and the frames we can see a beginning and an end: they can contain holes, niches or protuberances. In the length of the perimeter we can see the relationship with the context: the walls and the frames can be expanded, compressed or interrupted. Each place and each building has a favourite material: wood, metal, brick, plaster, glass, stone, concrete. The choice belongs to the essence of the idea, never coming after the formal definition of the building. The building draws its strength from the precise form which the material makes inevitable.

Maybe Gullichsen is a cannibal who steals and savagely reutilizes what he loves; perhaps Kairamo repeatedly endeavours to build the same building pursuing a chimera of modernism; it may be that Vormala believes the soul of the project should lie in constructive logic and in the worthiness of the mean quality. But for all three of them it is true that every construction should build its own image and identify itself ironically with its own modern function: country home, fire station, shopping centre, city home, industry, skyscraper, museum. Without however forgetting their ancestors: hut, church, sauna, farm, village, market, palace, tower, plant.

The chimney is often a discreet actor of the buildings, because it knows it is always necessary. Looking at it with an inquisitive eye, we find it well designed and strategically located: it is a sign both functional and symbolic inviting us to come in, sit together, have a drink and treat architecture like an old chum.

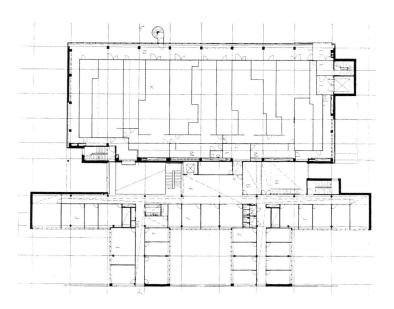

Houses

To really work, homes should be something more than being mere houses, and should let themselves be possessed by whoever lives in them. They should be simple, rational places. It was with that twofold objective in mind that over the last thirty years Kristian Gullichsen, Erkki Kairamo and Timo Vormala carried out a large corpus of housing designs. Whether they be city or vacation houses, flats or villas, terraced or row houses, the heart of the matter has always been the same: not solving a problem of numbers or repetition, but creating conditions for the design to grow and be enriched over the years. Kairamo clearly expressed that concept in the designs executed at Westend in the early 1980s, where each frame has a different function in modulating the transition between public and private spheres; each frame is both structure and decoration.

The small homes the three Finnish architects have built for themselves or for their clients reflect the heroic dimension of dwelling, in the hope that in a beautiful house comfort and adventure can effectively coincide. A home is above all a shelter enabling us to relate with the topography of the land. That is what we see in the Hanikka Houses at Espoo, in the Petite Maison in Grasse, in the Villa Aulikki in the Turku archipelago, but also in the Lyökkiniemi middle-class homes at Westend and at Meritähti. At will, we can live in a modern palafitte, in the thickness of a dry-stone wall, in a makeshift hut, or else in the elegant reinterpretation of a 1930s' ship. On the other hand, in the high-density residential districts Vormala designed in Helsinki over the last ten years, a typically Scandinavian realism prevails, a value enhanced by the recognisability of each individual site: the right scale and light, large and top-quality windows, terraces that purposely look onto something, the line of the perimeter that physically defines the boundary space, a clear distinction between outside and inside space. The two Olympos Urban villas have the privilege of looking onto the Helsinki ferry harbour; in defining a small stronghold, they seem to ask us: 'Is there really a difference between a village and a city? Or are they not the same thing, but at different moments of their long life?'

Erkki Kairamo
Maija Kairamo

Hanikka Houses
Espoo, 1970

On the two
previous pages:
Näkinpuisto Apartment
block, Helsinki.
Exterior street view.

First floor plan,
longitudinal section,
side elevation.

Exterior view.

The original designs included for five detached houses on a coastal site 20 km east of Helsinki, of which only two were constructed.

The buildings were designed as longitudinal prisms whose ends open out to the sea; the level differences in the rising shoreline allowed for a two-storey design with a high living room, library balconies and terraces facing south. The garage and equipment stores form a small entrance courtyard from which the building is entered on the main level. At midstage of the prism the entrance corridor opens out into a double-height space in which the dining areas, library and studies are on the upper level overlooking the living room and master bedrooms on the lower. The sauna and storage spaces are also situated on the lower level, cut into the slope.

The intention was to give the buildings a light, villa-like impression. These buildings were Erkki Kairamo´s first independent works, and they, together with a sauna building he designed ten years previously for his mother on the same plot, are clearly a strand in his lifelong theme and methodical constructivism. The structure is a composite lattice of steel stanchions and timber beams, whose infill is of formply wall panels. Because of the building system and on the wishes of the clients, both houses appear to be very similar, but on closer inspection each has its own individual character, one hallmarked by rational utility, the other a dynamic home for artistic sensibilities.

Thirty years have passed since completion, and the buildings are still in good condition lodged in tranquillity and a haven of greenery.

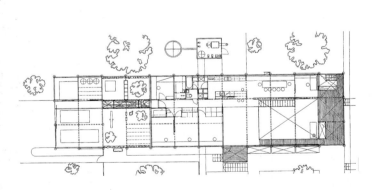

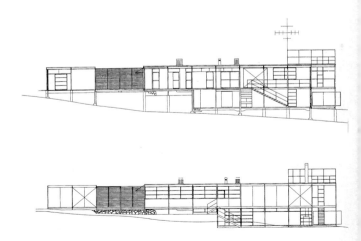

Exterior view of the
two-floor loggia.

Interior view
of the double-height
living room.

Kristian Gullichsen

La Petite Maison
Grasse, France, 1972

Exterior perspective.

Exterior view of the house
set in the stone terraces.

The Petite Maison, situated in a terraced olive plantation in Southern France, was conceived not to stand out, but to disappear in the landscape.

Consequently, the structure was integrated in the pre-existent architecture of stone terraces.

There is no formal main entrance to the building — all rooms in the bazaar-like structure o-pen the main space — the adjoining terrace with its swimming pool and to the bucolic Mediterranean landscape.

It is a very intimate house, more suitable for the lifestyle of a contemporary Diogenes than for formal socialising; everything is private.

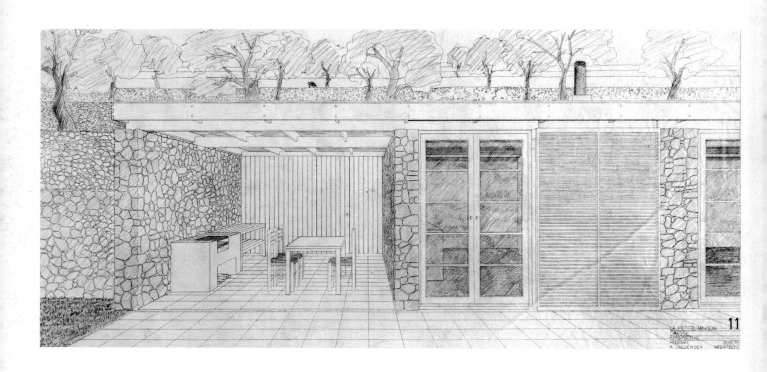

Interior view
of the living room.

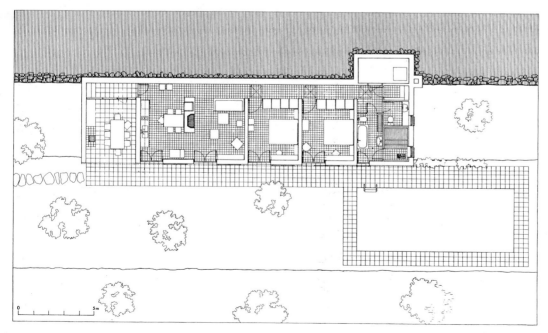

Plan with the open loggia
to the left and
the swimming pool
to the right.

0   5m

Exterior view.

Erkki Kairamo

Liinasaarenkuja
Semi-detached houses
Westend, Espoo, 1982

Preliminary sketch.

The architectural language of this group of ten double houses echoes the white functionalist villas from the time when the residential area of Westend was developed in the thirties.

The concept is of the utmost simplicity, regular boxes of prefabricated concrete panels, structurally basic: houses of cards.

An additional layer of accessories — porches, balconies, fences and trellises — projecting from the boxes play a contrasting architectural game, which with the help of planting and trees have transformed the plain austerity of the ensemble into a Garden of Eden.

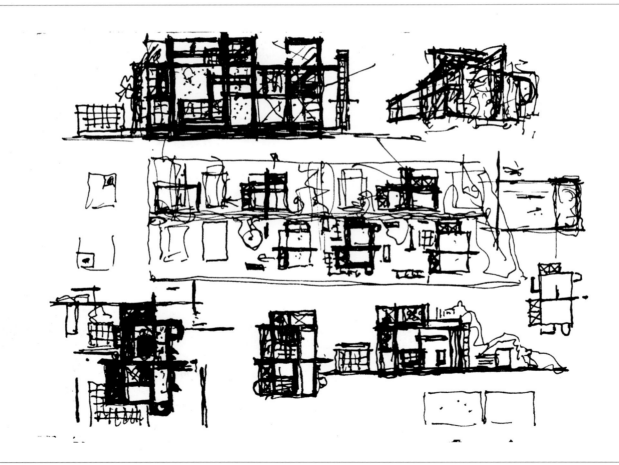

Site plan.

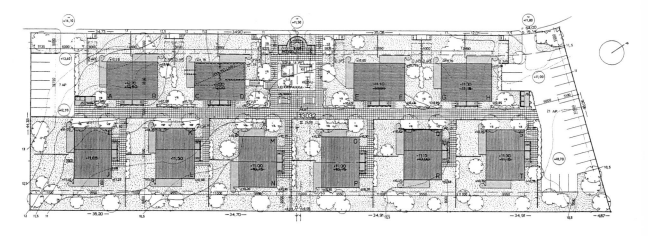

The south-facing
veranda of a house.

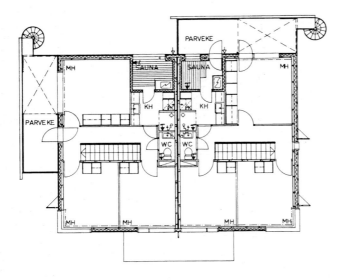

Typical first-floor plan.

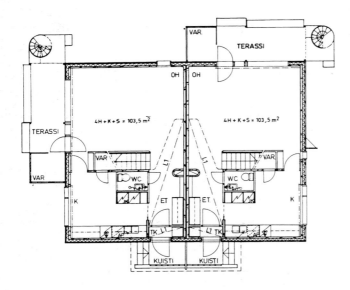

Typical first-floor plan.

Typical ground-floor plan.

View of the interior
pedestrian alley.

Almost twenty years
after construction,
the houses have been
taken over by the plants,
as originally intended.

Preliminary sketches.

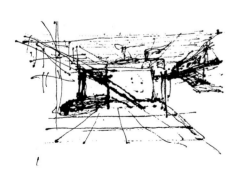

Hiiralankaari Apartment block
Espoo, Westend, 1983

View of the back
elevation.

Site plan.

Frontal view of the main
elevation, a composition
of balconies, terraces
and loggias.

This block of flats in the Westend seaside suburb
is a straightforward structure assembled from pre-
fabricated concrete panels.

The rear elevation of the building with its
strip windows mirrors the logic of the prefab system.

The main facade overlooking the sea is articulated with a zone of in situ concrete balconies
whose structural independence frees them from
the rigidity of the block, enabling a contrapuntal
play of irregularities to contrast with the main body
of the building.

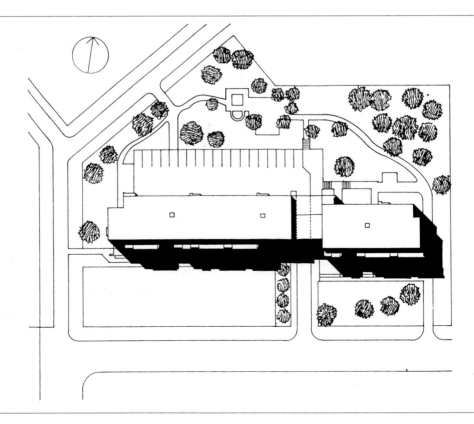

View of the main
elevation, combining
structural and
temporary elements.

Floor plans.
From bottom to top: first,
second and third.

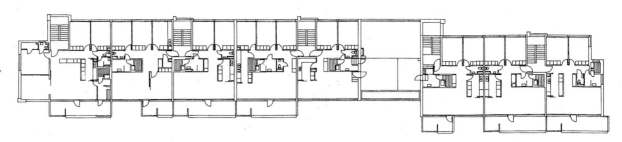

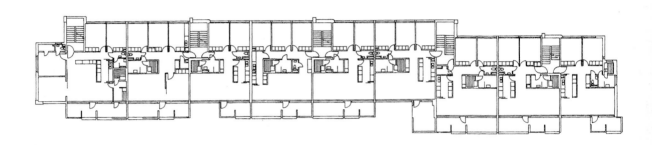

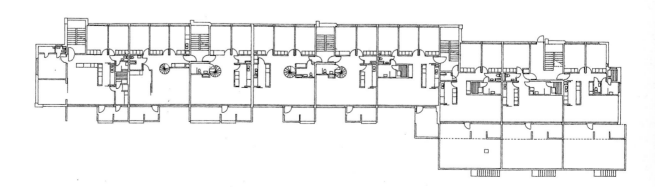

Erkki Kairamo

Lyökkiniemi Semi-detached houses
Espoo, Westend, 1990

Site plan, with the road
access to the left and
the sea to the right.

Of the residential designs by Erkki Kairamo in the affluent suburb of Westend, a 15 minute drive from the centre of Helsinki, this is the last, and the only one to occupy a precious seafront site.

The building is divided by a wall into two symmetrical units, each facing the sea and sharing the same garden. The main spaces, designed both as dining and living rooms, extend to face both the sea to the north and the intimate kitchen courtyards on the south side. The libraries are double-height spaces which reach from the ground to the sleeping quarters on the first floor. The basement contains saunas, swimming pools and utility spaces.

The architectural vocabulary is in faithful accordance with the author's commitment to the modern tradition; there are no deviations from the narrow path.

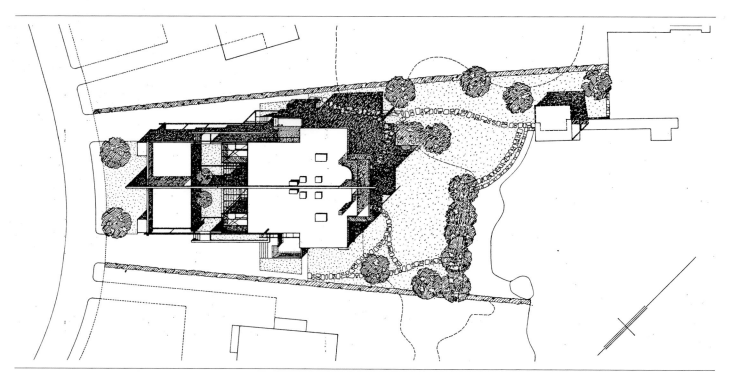

Site plan, with the road access to the left and the sea to the right.

Preliminary sketches.

Floor plans. From bottom
to top: basement,
ground and first.

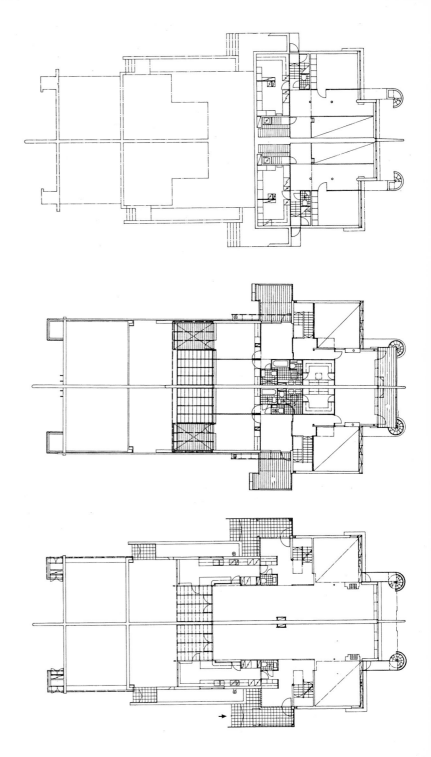

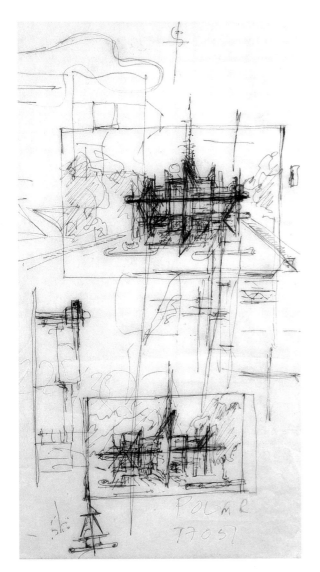

Side view,
with the garages
to the left
and the entrance
to the right, and the sea
in the back.

Side elevation and
longitudinal section.

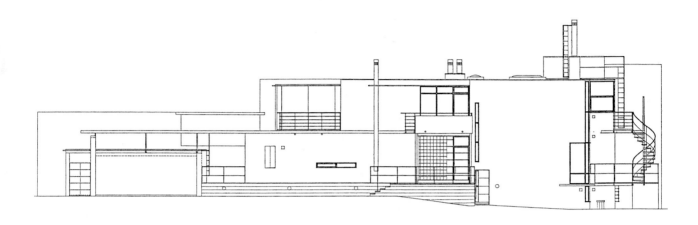

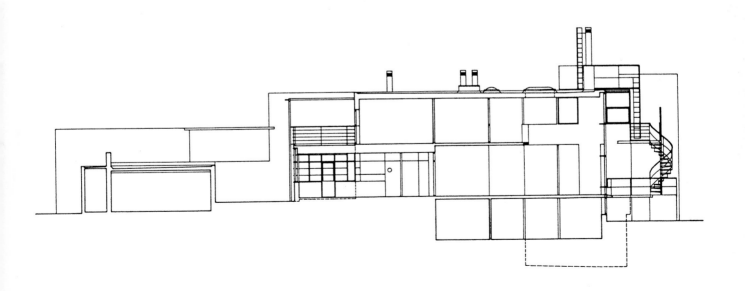

Side view of the front
elevation, with the spiral
staircase connecting to
the bedroom level and
the living room window.

Construction drawing
of the entrance
glass-brick wall.

Views of the ground floor
kitchen courtyard, and
of the living room window
overlooking the sea.

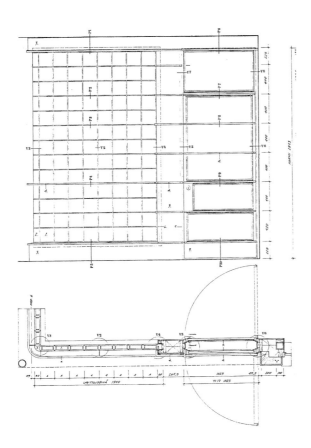

49

View of the front
elevation.

Preliminary sketch.

Erkki Kairamo
Aulikki Jylhä

Villa Aulikki
Halskär, 1994

Sketch showing the
chimney, the outside table
and tent, the mast
and the stones.

For twenty years Erkki Kairamo spent his summers sailing in the archipelago of the Gulf of Finland. In 1986 he bought small windswept rocky island there, whose only existing structure was a small fishing hut of 6m2, which, for one used to the strictures of space on a sailing boat, was an adequate summer base.

Further space was necessary, however, for all-year round existence: sleeping and living quarters and storage. Over the long design period the problems and aims remained the same, a 'non-building' as unobtrusive as possible from the sea; a low, flat roofed of 15m2 linked to the existing structure via a courtyard. The whole structure is supported against a rock face and the grey weathered timbers blend in with the background. A sail is suspended over the terrace as a summer canopy.

In summer 1994, prior to his death, Erkki Kairamo completed his designs, from which his remaining family has since begun construction.

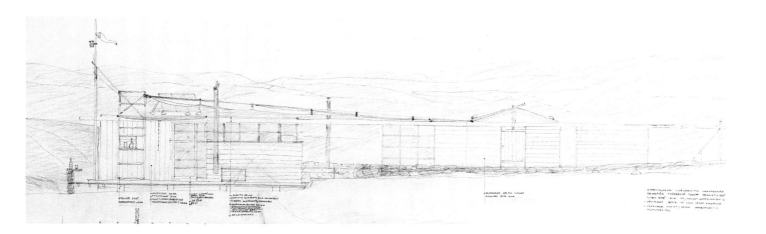

Sketch of the side
elevation.

Overall view.

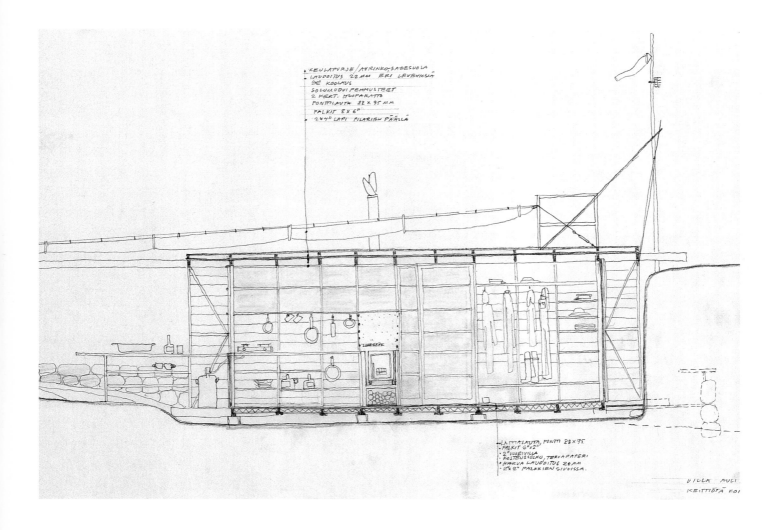

Perspective sketch.

Exterior view.

Kristian Gullichsen

Olympos Urban villas
Myllytie, Helsinki, 1995

Site plan.

View of the exterior
entrance space forming
a courtyard between
the two buildings.

The residential complex occupies a unique park-like site on a hill overlooking the inner harbour of the city.

The completed project, based on a winning competition entry, consists of two urban villas, each containing six flats designed for lease to executives and diplomats. The villas are connected by an underground parking garage.

The basement also accommodates sauna and swimming pool facilities with access to a discreet outdoor terrace.

The apartments range in size from two to five-room units. Generous balconies and penthouse terraces with steel canopies offer panoramic views over the city and the sea.

The complex has two faces. The vertically accented massing facing the harbour reflects the dynamism of the setting, whilst on the side of the inner access court at the top of the hill, the scale and the expression is calm and intimate, the abstract white rendering of the walls turns into a warm yellow.

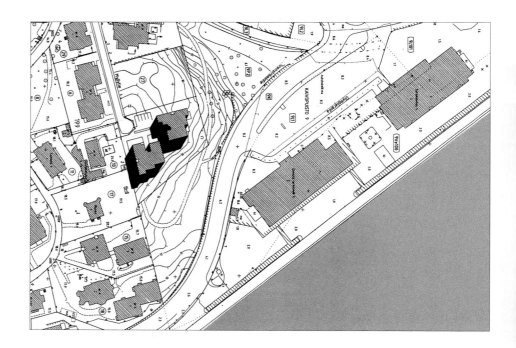

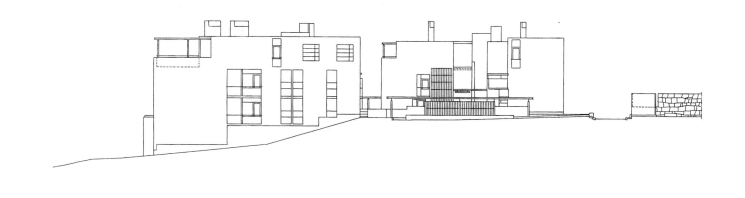

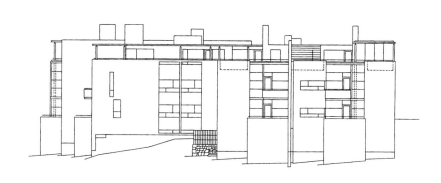

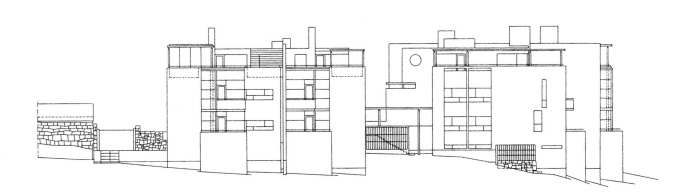

Elevations.

Ground floor plan.

Second floor plan.

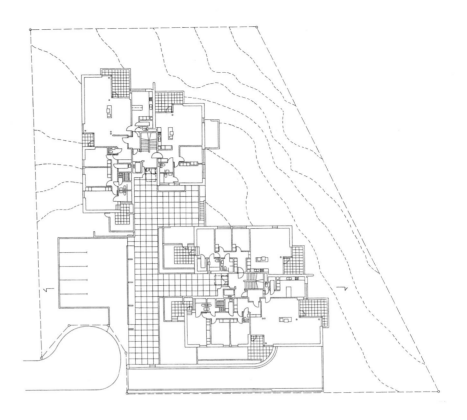

The sinuous alcove
forming a seat next to the
entry door of one of the
buildings. View and plan.

View of the rear elevation
overlooking the inner
harbour.

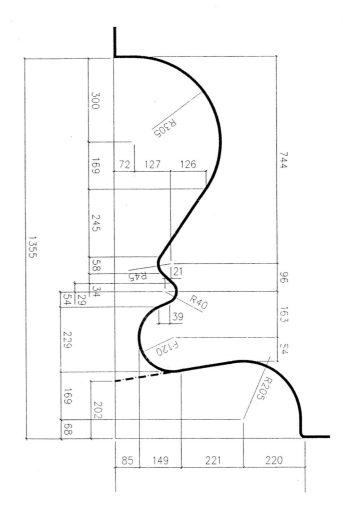

Timo Vormala

Meritähti Apartments
Helsinki, 1997

Site plan showing the
three tower blocks and
the terrace houses.

The overwhelming asset of the site is its location on an area of extensive parkland bordering the sea and the tremendous views which open out from its high situation; the solution is based on making maximum use of these factors.

The siting and forms of the buildings were strictly controlled by the town plan for the area, which had been pieced together over a number of years; our efforts were largely directed at the internal organisation of the complex.

The project consisted of an unusually large privately-funded residential group, and prospective buyers were given the opportunity of limited participation with regard to the size, amount of rooms and level of fitted-furnishing in their future homes.

The basic storey plan comprises a succession of spaces wrapped around an internal stairwell. In-situ column and slab construction made possible the division into four apartment lots, each different in size. The corners of the plan are reserved for large glazed balconies.

For the standard floors ten different apartment layouts ranging from 55-137m2 were designed, which, by combining with each other in various combinations, produced a range of different storey layouts. Two large apartments with roof terraces are situated on the uppermost floor.

The stairwells are a direct link from the apartments to the exterior ground level and to two subterranean levels of parking; a glazed light-well extending above the building relieves the impression of confinement within, and, lit both day and night is a link from inside to outside and a rooftop beacon to the exterior world.

Roof terraces are also provided for the use of all inhabitants — even those living at a lower level can enjoy the magnificent sea views.

Three-storey row houses as demanded by the area plan are sheltered by the towers and their lack of views towards the sea is compensated by provision a small garden for each dwelling.

The buildings, characterised by maritime associations, have sleek white prefabricated elevations, decks, balconies with railings and a flagpole construction indicative of the navigating bridge, reminders of the golden age of seafaring.

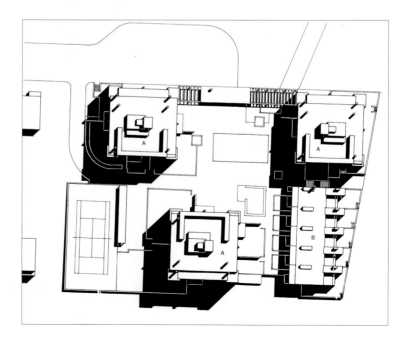

The terrace houses seen
from the upper floor
balconies of the tower
blocks.

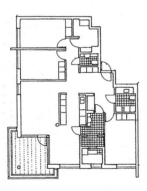

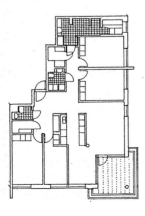

Tower blocks. Different
possible apartment
configurations at different
corners.
View of a side elevation.

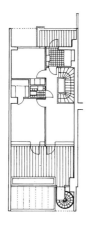

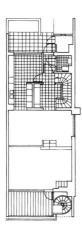

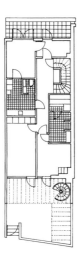

Terrace houses. From
bottom to top: ground,
first and second floor
plans.

View of the front
elevation.

Timo Vormala

Kesäkatu Apartment block
Helsinki, 1999

Site plan, with the sea
on the right.

The group of buildings is situated along the boundary of an extensive urban park close to the sea. Its elevations have a strong directionality to take advantage of the magnificent sea views.

The largest apartments, which have ample balconies, roof terraces or fireplaces, have been located on the upper three floors.

The buiding's architectural expression is, on the one hand, guided by maritime association, and on the other is evocative of pavilions in the park from a previous era.

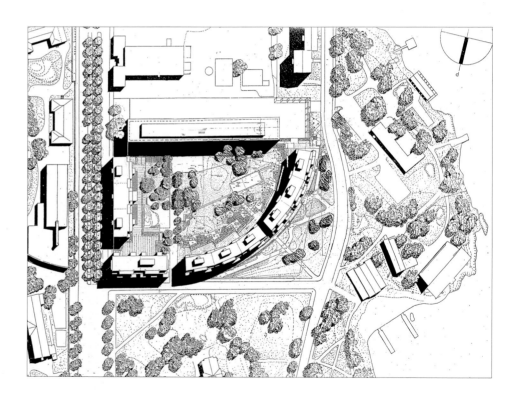

The exterior facade of the
crescent.

Top left: on the sixth floor, two 128.5 sqm apartments.
Top right: on the seventh floor, two 104.5 sqm apartments.
Bottom left: from the first to the fourth floors, two 96.5 sqm and one 63.5 sqm apartments.
Bottom right: on the fifth floor, two 128.5 sqm apartments.

The interior facade of the crescent.

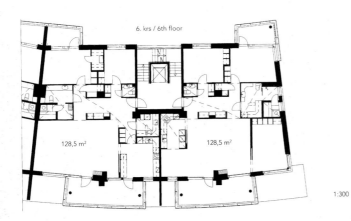

6. krs / 6th floor

128,5 m²   128,5 m²

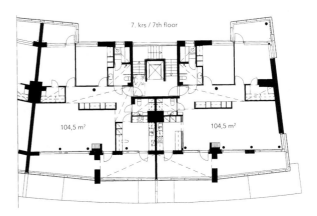

7. krs / 7th floor

104,5 m²   104,5 m²

1:300

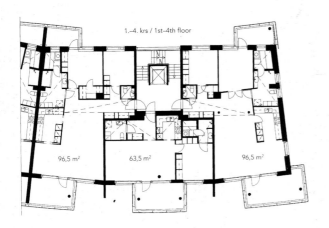

1.–4. krs / 1st–4th floor

96,5 m²   63,5 m²   96,5 m²

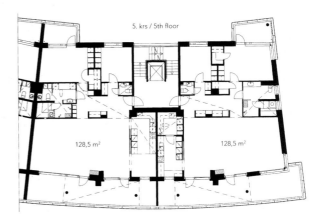

5. krs / 5th floor

128,5 m²   128,5 m²

Industrial world

At Varkaus, in the great lakes region, two volumes, laid out in an L-shape, compose an industrial district; thanks to the disposition of the shapes and materials, they have become synonymous of the city centre. The designers — and here Erkki Kairamo's contribution is clearly legible — rightly considered industry as architecture for its own sake and as a vibrant part of the city, providing it with the formal and symbolic meanings that are usually associated with other types of buildings. The paper mill and its power plant, far from forming a dull background, are proud urban protagonists: they unaffectedly represent the productive activities that are consumed within the envelope, and their facades are an essay on building techniques. The main purpose of the overall design is to make the two aspects coincide, so the order of the production line mirrors the order of the architectural construction, and not the reverse, as is often the case in hi-tech architecture. The long horizontal element, the chimneystacks, the metal stairways, the glass walls, and the cold precision of the details, make it such an exemplary ensemble that it nearly makes us long for the reassuring presence of an industry in the city.

Two experimental designs, connected with the theme of pre-fabrication, prove empirically that we can use technology without being overpowered by it. The former, Moduli, deals with the theme of modular wooden houses, while the latter, Urban Housing Prototypes, with the use of window profiles. Reduced to bare essentials, the components of the two systems express a broad range of configurations, and can be fashioned in one, two or three dimensions, or else in lines, planes or volumes. We might call it an artisanal use of technology.

The Espoo Fire station, with its manifold dimensions, perfectly describes the concept of a building technique that is form as well: it is a dissertation about beauty, about pathos and about the compositional possibilities of structure, of screens, and of building accessories, while remaining in the sphere of simplicity. Here the forces and weights of the materials are clearly legible, and inside each piece we perceive the why and the how of each choice, and actually touch that symbiosis blending form and function in a single artifact.

Kristian Gullichsen
Juhani Pallasmaa

Moduli 225
1968–73

On the two previous pages: Marimekko textile works, Helsinki. Exterior view of the details.

The horizontal and vertical components, and the principal assembly joint.

A major industrial company in Finland commissioned the architects to develop a new product for their factory producing wooden prefab houses.

The Moduli 225 is a holiday house system, a do-it-yourself kit-of-parts based on factory finished elements. The dimensions and details of joints are co-ordinated to facilitate the combination of elements in a number of ways within the cubic post and beam frame. The key detail solutions are the adjustable foundation and the aluminium connector which structurally stiffens the frame allowing however easy dismantling, re-erection and extension. The weight limit of 50 kilos for any element was determined to allow easy transportation and erection by manual labour without the use of heavy machinery. Regrettably, the factory was closed down at the time the system was tested and ready for mass production.

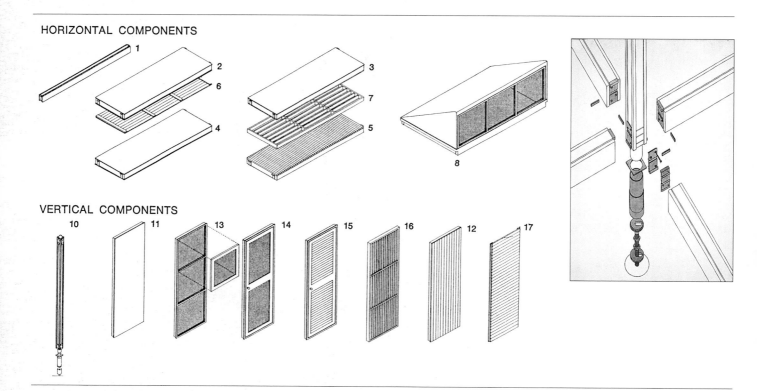

HORIZONTAL COMPONENTS

VERTICAL COMPONENTS

The assembly
of the structural elements.

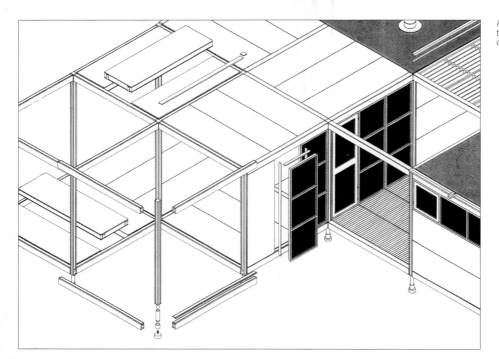

Axonometric showing
the assembly
of the components.

Looking from
the outside towards
the interior.

Looking from
the interior towards
the outside.

The variety of possible
configurations.

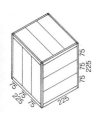
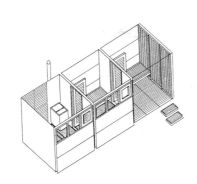
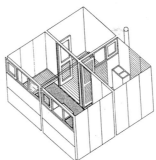
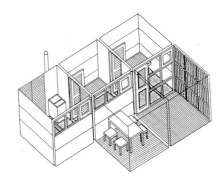

Perspective sketch.

An entire village made
of Moduli units.

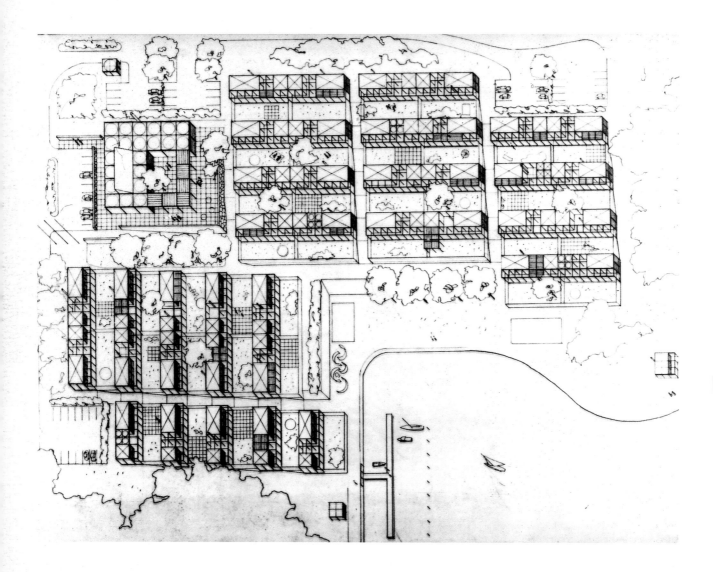

Erkki Kairamo

Paper mill
Varkaus, 1977

Site plan with the
entrance building
at the top left corner.

The mill manufacturing printing paper is an extension to an important industrial complex located in the vast district of forests and interconnected lakes in Central Finland. Strong emphasis was placed on the environmental issues, both ecological and architectural.

Architecturally the challenge was how to fit the vast structure on a narrow strip of land between a lake and the city centre, the problem of scale being the major concern since the new plant is about one-kilometre long.

The implemented design strategy was to break down the massive structure by articulating the characteristic features of the industrial process. Extensive use of glass in the facades provides ample daylight to the interiors and, as the mill is running day and night, the interior lighting illuminates the darkness of the long Nordic winter.

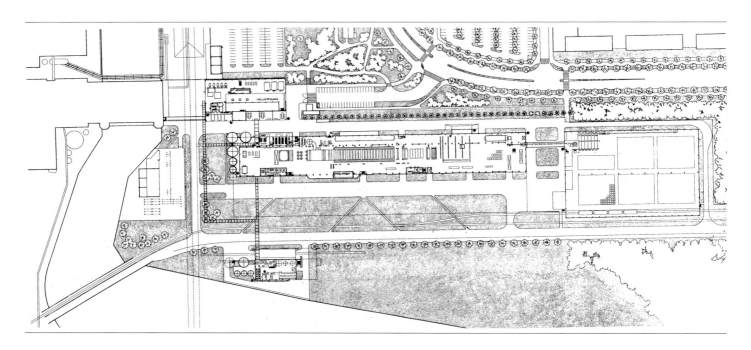

The Paper mill seen from
the entrance building
rooftop.

The Paper mill seen from
the water-side.

Cross section.
The entrance building
is on the right and the
water is on the left.

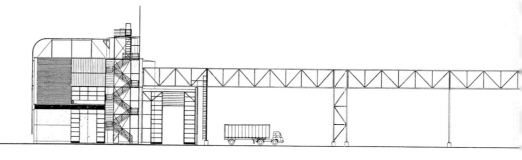

The meeting corner
of the Paper mill (left)
and the entrance building
(right).

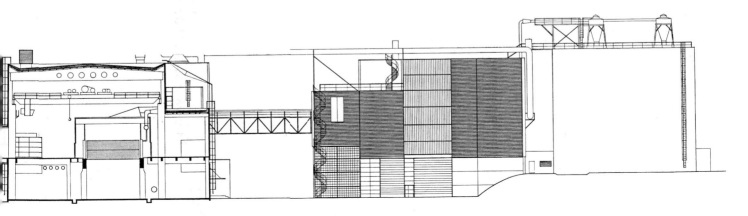

The land-side elevation.

The interior space.

Erkki Kairamo

Power plant
Varkaus, 1990

Site plan, with the Power
plant at the top left
corner.

The front elevation facing
the access road
from the centre of town.

In the 1970s a zone occupied by the new paper-manufacturing units became part of the town centre of Varkaus. With the increase in energy demand a new power plant became necessary, and this was constructed to supply steam and electric power to the manufacturing process. The new boiler runs on solid fuel, i.e., coal and timber waste material with two separate conveyor systems.

The main design problem was how to merge the large boiler building (44 m high and 27 m wide), the electrostatic filter and the conveyors with the townscape. Together with the process design, the building mass was organised vertically to combine the demands of both function and townscape. The accented equipment-lifting well, stairs, air-conditioning ducts and conveyors form a network of vertical, horizontal and oblique lines which reflect the function of the building. The use of glass as the main material alongside sheetmetal surfaces makes the building less massive and links it to the adjacent paper mill, forming a coherent unit of industrial buildings bound by the town centre.

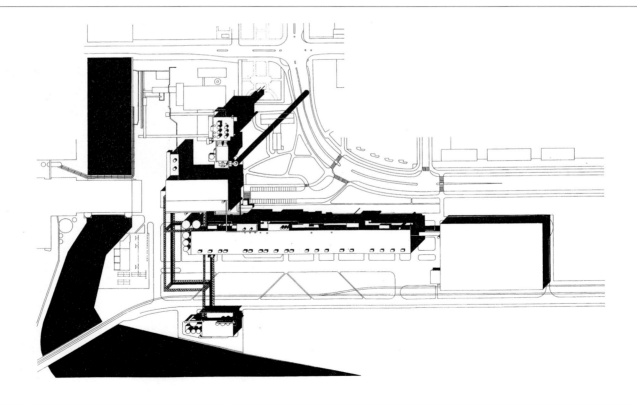

The back elevation
facing the waterway.

Elevation facing
the centre of town.

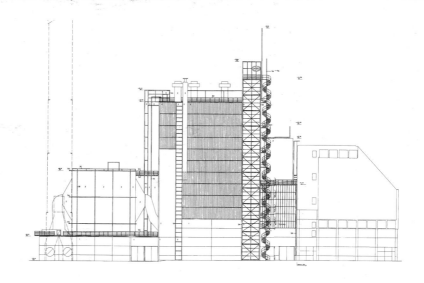

Longitudinal section.

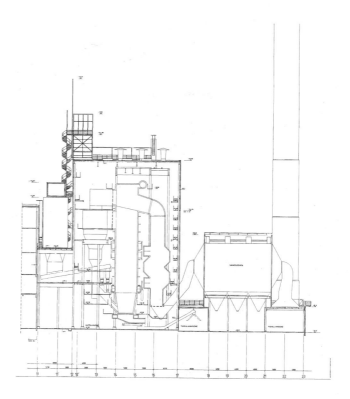

View from the bottom up
of the catwalks serving
the boiler building.

Exterior view
of the boiler building.

Erkki Kairamo

Fire station
Espoo, 1991

Site plan.

The top part
of the exterior
staircase tower.

The notion of dynamism appears as a recurring theme throughout the entire architectural work of Erkki Kairamo.

With the commission to design a Fire station he received a perfect opportunity to express direction and movement not as an architectural abstraction but as a direct response to the logic of the task.

Three items of the programme stand out in the visual impact of the design: the fire engines, the firemen's poles and the tower. The fire engines wait behind large transparent automatic doors, the fire poles at both ends of twin corridors connect the staff area on the first floor with the vehicle room below or with the outdoor area.

The fire tower, which is no longer the traditional place for drying hoses, serves a variety of training needs, e.g. equipment handling and rescues via ladder, stair, balconies or windows. Fixed to the Lissitzky-like tower are the station's code number and various technical installations such as a wind sock, anemometer and an antenna.

The architectural language of the boxlike volume, articulated with Kairamo's personal constructivist vocabulary, is consistently in accordance with the practical demand of a fire station and generates an appropriate, visually strong expression.

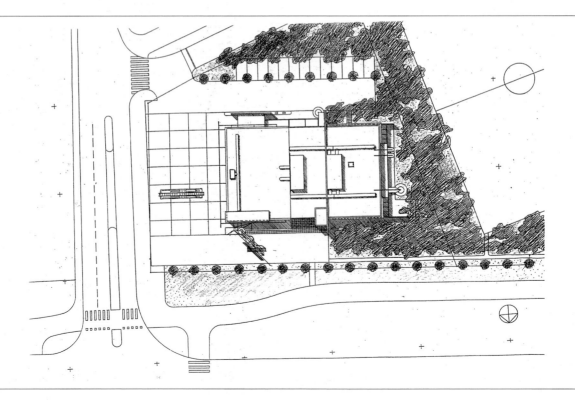

The exterior staircase
tower: overall view
and elevation.

Ground floor plan.

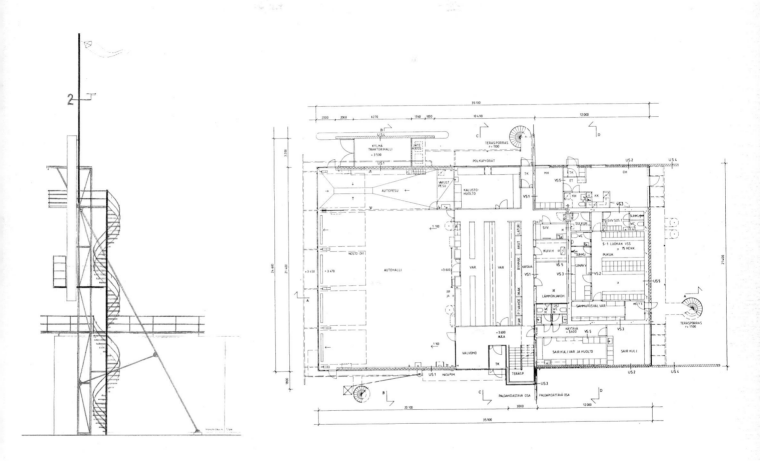

Corner view;
the external staircase acts
as a hinge between
the two elevations.

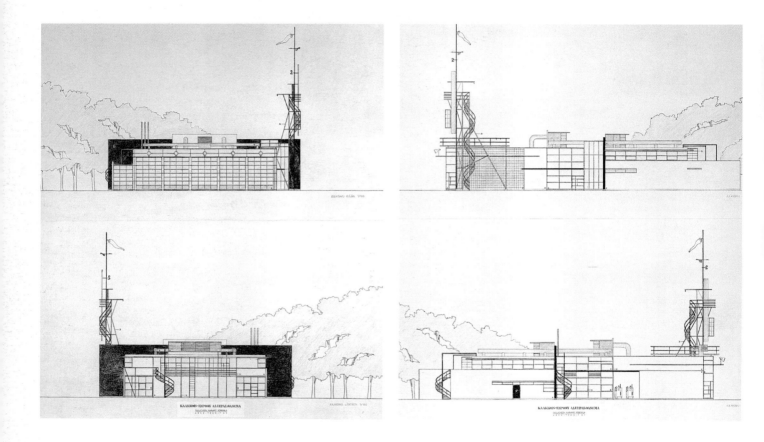

Kristian Gullichsen

Urban housing prototype
1992

Cut-away perspective,
showing the
outside/inside
relationship.

The well-known Swiss steel tube manufacturer Jansen and the leading German plate glass manufacturer Vegla asked an international group of architects to develop steel-glass constructions under the theme 'Transparent Spaces'. Our contribution was adopted to an urban housing prototype with duplex apartments and double height winter gardens.

The *fin du siècle* theme of glass-enclosed intermediate zones between internal and external space is, by the closing of this century, once again appearing as a major architectural motif.

Sophisticated structural systems together with the perfection of glass technology provide a host of new design options as well as improved possibilities of controlling climatic conditions.

Our contribution to the Steel-Glass Workshop was however not based on an ambition to ex-

plore the limits of technology. On the contrary, it is a low-key implementation of the present range of standard profiles, which do provide quite reasonable possibilities of designing technically proven, cost efficient and handsome structures. In other words, the aim was not to present any 'innovations', but to make good use of the accumulated experience in the field of building with steel and glass. The ecological imperative gives us every reason not to reinvent the wheel, but to recirculate current know-how as long as it is technically and economically valid.

The same principle was adopted in the scheme as a whole; the presented urban housing prototype is a reinterpretation of Le Corbusier's 'Pavillon de l'Esprit Nouveau' presented in 1925, but still adequate today as a concept for contemporary lifestyles.

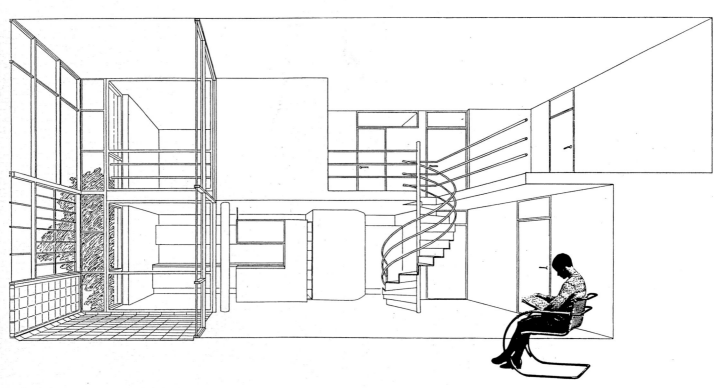

View of the model.

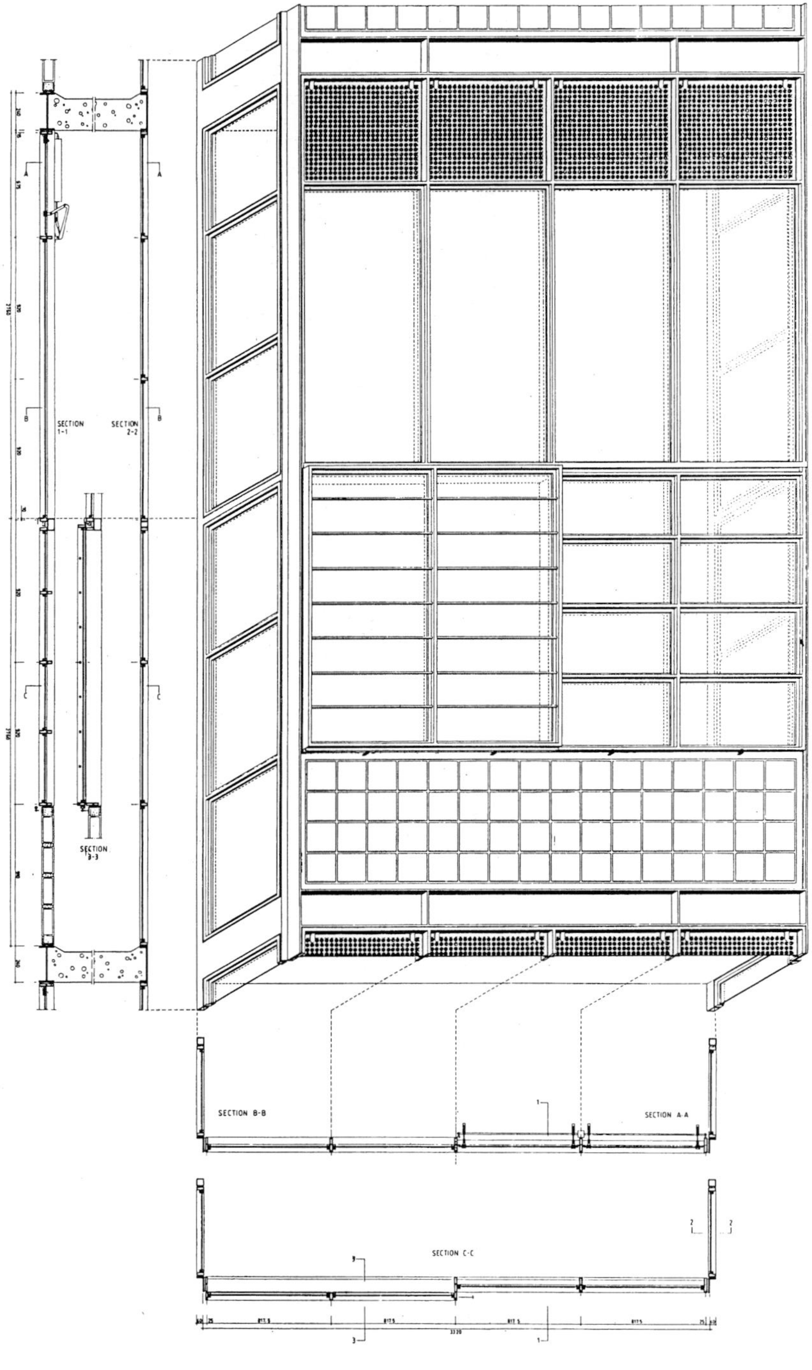

Plan, section
and isometric
of the window.

SECTION
1-1

SECTION
2-2

SECTION
3-3

SECTION B-B

SECTION A-A

SECTION C-C

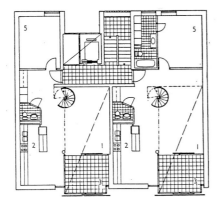

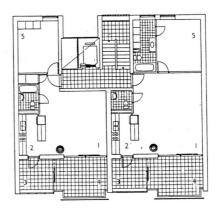

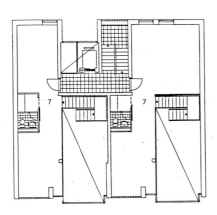

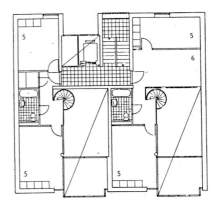

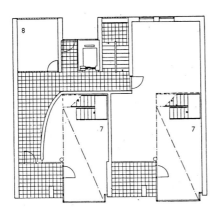

Left column,
from bottom to top:
ground, first, second
and fourth floor.
Right column,
from bottom to top:
third and fifth floor,
penthouse.
Legend:
1. Living room
2. Kitchen
3. Winter garden
4. Terrace
5. Bedroom
6. Multipurpose
7. Commercial
or office space
8. Storage

Public buildings

Public buildings reveal two fundamental rules of the Kristian Gullichsen, Erkki Kairamo and Timo Vormala design method. On the one hand, recovering that aura of sacrality and mystery characteristic of the public buildings of the past that, adulterated over the years, in our day is often held to be lost. On the other, conceiving those buildings as places not only to go to, but to stay in, hence capable of slowing down the flow of time. The functions of the four buildings (a Parish centre and a Civic centre in Finland, a University library in Spain, an Embassy in Sweden) are not immediately obvious, but are intentionally kept concealed, so you can even sense a certain resemblance in the forms.

Kristian Gullichsen, the author of those designs, only two of which are fully built up to now, describes them as being made up of parts, since each contains a progression made of various perceptive experiences. At Kauniainen, the Parish centre features a columbarium, a rising stairway, a lateral path, and then a glass partition forming the winding entrance, a balcony, the space of the church with its geometric skylights, and a green pergola. The Pieksämäki Civic centre has walls in various materials arranged in different forms, with the addition of monumental entrances, a romantic fireplace, a whimsical tower and a veranda for the summer months. At the Lleida University library, a full-height portico connects the facade on the street to the inner courtyard: this contains balconies, stairways, loggias, screens, taperings in the walls and sloping glass windows, an entire abacus of situations. Each one of these works unwinds on the ground as if it were a rope, and opposes one facade to the other: thus other perceptions arise and new points of view unfold, often picturesque in character.

In these designs, function and fiction coincide, play and gravity overlap. They transmit that *joie de vivre* and that spatial generosity that enabled Finnish architecture to grow and play a guiding role in democratic society. In the details and in the composition of parts one perceives a tribute to Mediterranean architecture and climate.

Kristian Gullichsen
Eeva Kilpiö

Parish centre
Kauniainen, 1979–99

On the two previous
pages: Geodetic Institute,
Masala, Kirkkonummi.
Exterior view.

Located on a hillside in a small town neighbouring
Helsinki, the scheme — the result of a competition
in 1978 — includes a 200-seater church, a number of separate meeting rooms, and an administra-
tive wing.

The complex, completed in 1983, forms, together with an existing chapel and kindergarten
wing (Keijo Petäjä, 1964), a closed courtyard do-
minated by a slim bell tower also designed by
Petäjä.

In 1999 the original kindergarten wing was
replaced with a new structure, and a columbarium
with access from the lower end of the slope was
constructed. The volume of the original building
and its role in the overall composition were however
retained.

The horizontal wall-like entrance facade of
the main building continued round the corner as a
red-brick rampart constitutes a physical and psychological barrier to the busy secular environment,
creating a silent cloister-like world inside.

The cubic volumes, the hilltown street motif,
the white-walled piazza with its portico and campa-
nile, are reflections of the Mediterranean origins of
Christianity as are the fragments of classical herita-
ge — exedra variations, colonnades, pergolas etc.

The church hall, sunk into the hill, receives
daylight from above through rooflights and the cata-
comb-like access corridor recalls the underground
worship of early Christians. By contrast, the spirit of
the modern masters, Le Corbusier and Aalto, can be
identified without difficulty.

Site plan.

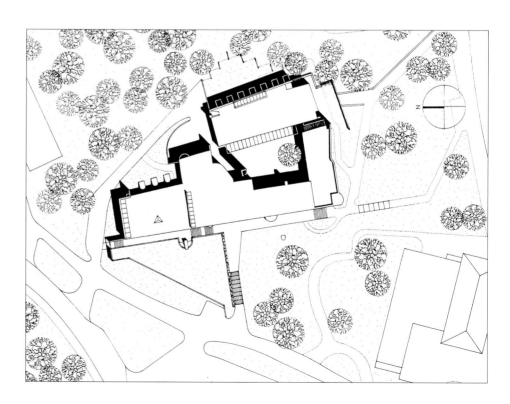

Ground floor plan.
Legend:
1. Vestibule
2. Church
3. Parish hall
4. Sacristy
5. Mortuary
6. Club room
7. Offices
8. Kindergarten
9. Void

First floor plan.
Legend:
1. Void
2. Void
3. Parish Hall
4. Kitchen
5. Club Room
6. Mechanical
7. Storage
8. Vicar
9. Offices

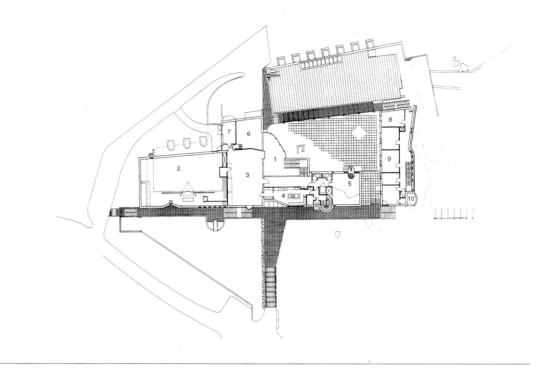

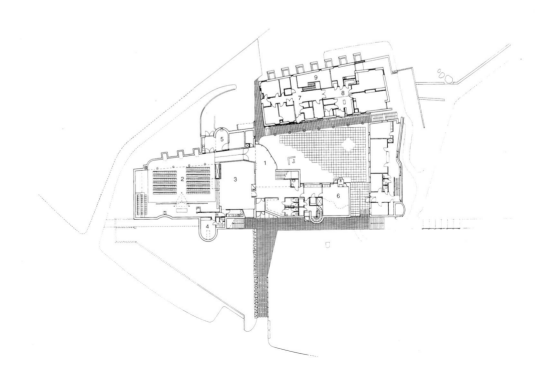

The processional side elevation.

The front elevation, whose blank walls provide a gap to view the bell-tower.

Longitudinal section, with
the church on the left.

Side view of the front
elevation. The skylights
serve the new
columbarium below
ground.

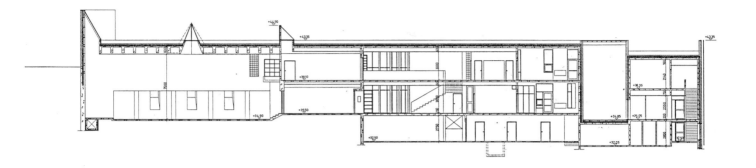

The trellis forming
a decoration
on the front facade.

The elements composing
the courtyard: the bell-
tower, the glazed wall,
the pathway, the pergola.

The church, with the
triangular skylight
indicating the altar.

Recessed windows
opposite the altar.

The underground
columbarium.
Interior view, plan
and section.

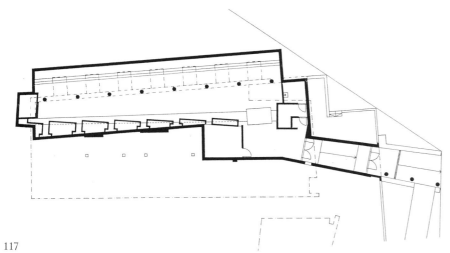

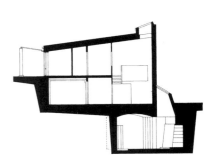

Kristian Gullichsen

Civic centre Poleeni
Pieksämäki, 1989

Site plan.

The building is situated in lakeshore parkland in Pieksämäki, a town in Central Finland. The scheme comprises the new city library, entrance hall with café, art gallery and a multipurpose auditorium seating 350. Its relaxed composition, which is derived from the peaceful lakeside setting, is a transitional element: with the urban milieu on one side and the parkland on the other, it acts both as a buffer against the street and a backdrop to the park. The tripartite street elevation contains echoes of a palazzo with entrance gate and courtyard — 'cour d'honneur'.

The long curving wall addressing the park stands aside from the landscape as an observer, surveying the scene with its large openings and projecting veranda. At the north end of the wall stands a watch-tower with moat, functioning as a children's story-room and reading area. This provides an apt setting for d'Artagnan, The Three Musketeers, William Tell, Robin Hood, and all the other characters who will inhabit the place.

The architectural language as a whole is a loose agglomeration of elements from many different origins, including classicism and functionalism. At a deeper level lies the tradition of some sixty-five years of the Modern Movement which we are trying to interpret. It is our conviction that this intellectual and artistic base contains an inexhaustible source of architectural concepts, rich in meaning and history. In short, it is a gold mine which it would be foolish not to explore.

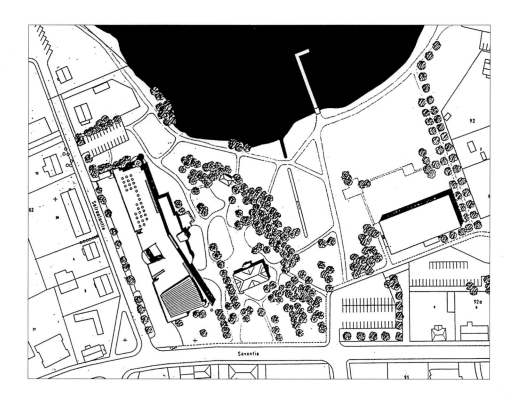

The town-side facade,
with the entry portal.

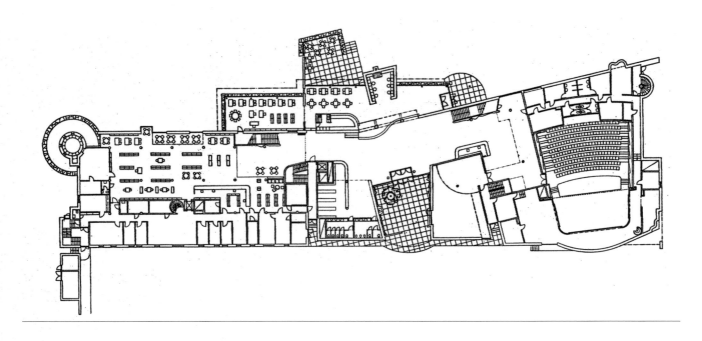

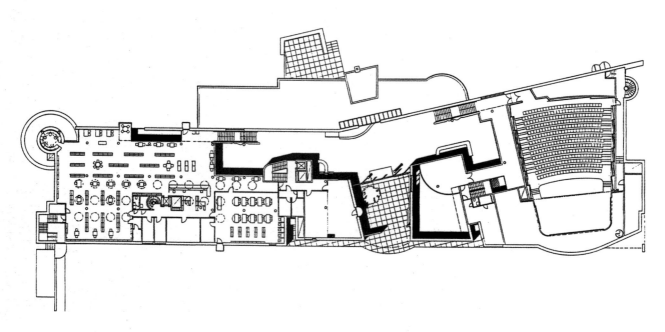

120

Ground floor
and first floor plans.

Elements of the town-side
facade: the entry portal,
the sinuous lines,
the corner portal.

Elements of the garden-
side facade: the Aaltian
canopy, the vernacular
stone wall, the Venetian
chimney.

The garden-side facade.

Cross-section through
the library.

Interior view. On the left,
the staircase to the first
floor library; on the right,
the entrance space;
in the back, the staircase
to the auditorium gallery.

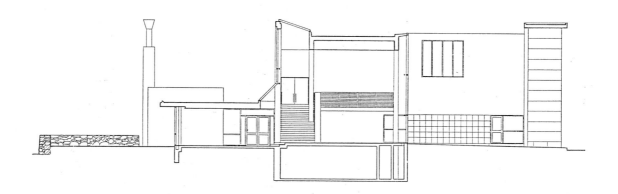

Children reading in the
library. A sketch by
Gullichsen: the analogy
between a shelf full
of books and a library
building.

The medieval corner
tower: exterior
and interior.

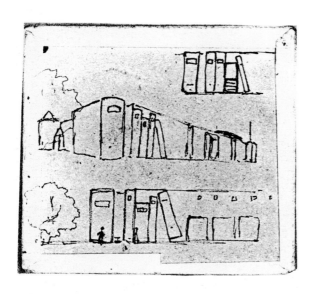

Sketches by Gullichsen:
the medieval corner tower
and the entrance court.

The sculptural staircase
leading to the library,
and the fireplace room
met upon entering
the building.

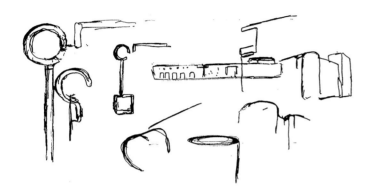

Kristian Gullichsen

The Embassy of Finland
Stockholm, Sweden, 1993–

Site plan.

The Embassy building, consisting of the Embassy's consular spaces and a separate residence wing, is situated on a restricted triangular site in the diplomatic quarter of Djurgården, opposite the Italian Cultural Institute by Gio Ponti.

The programme for the building also called for the inclusion of a banqueting hall, although the ambassador's official residence is situated in the centre of the city.

An embassy is not simply a normal office building, rather a public building representing its own nation abroad; in this design it has become a small palace complete with courtyards and gateways, an introverted concept expressing the ritual dignity of diplomacy and well suited for the security requirements of an embassy.

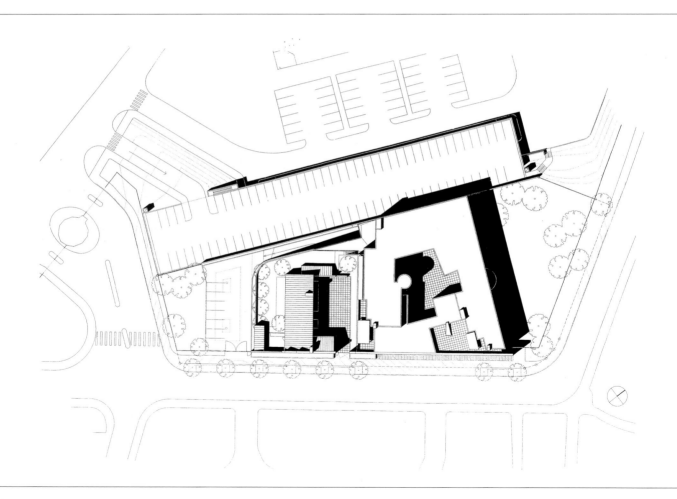

Perspective sketch
of the street facade.

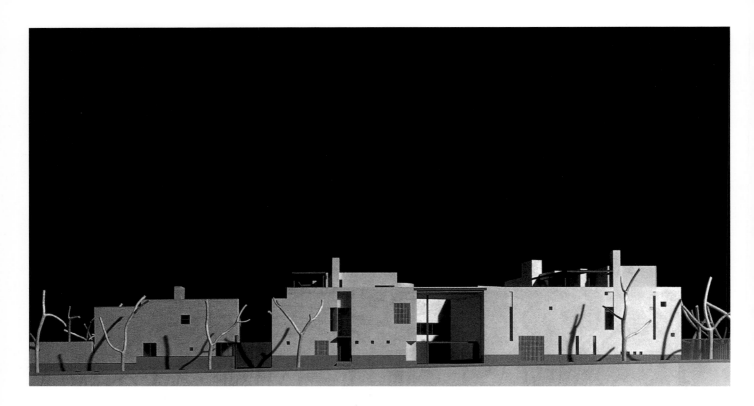

Street view of the model.

Ground floor plan.

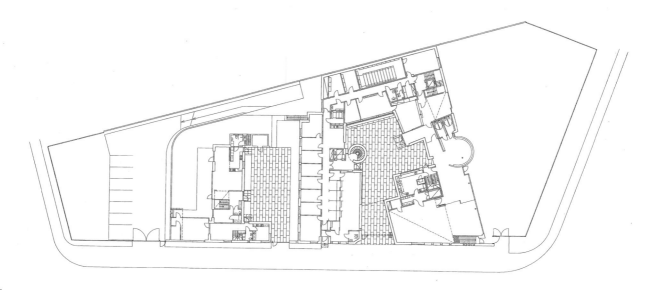

View of the model.

First floor plan.

Second floor plan.

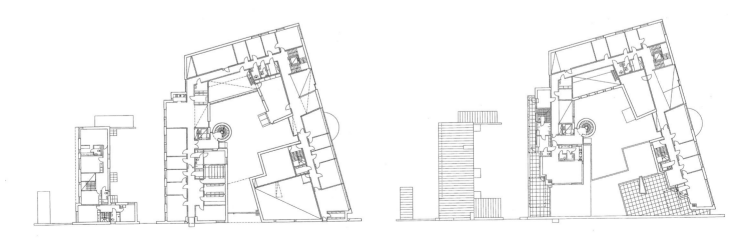

The street entrance.

The feast hall.

Kristian Gullichsen

University library
Lleida, Spain, 1996–

Cross-section through
the library block.

The model seen from
the courtyard side,
with the auditorium
on the right.

The Library project was initiated to celebrate the 700th anniversary of the Lleida University in Catalonia, Spain.

The scheme is based on the winning entry in an international competition in 1994. Construction works are scheduled to start in 1999 to complete the building within the first year of the new millennium.

The Library is expected to become the emblematic building of the new campus currently under construction on the left bank of river Segre in the proximity of the city centre.

The L-shaped complex in the corner of the new quarter will serve as an entrance gate to the university. The pedestrian route from the city centre (via a bridge) over the river to the campus area is focused under a large atrium, which will serve as a sheltered meeting point of the academic community and the society at large. The skew corner design reacts to the diagonal flow to and

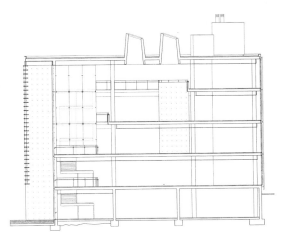

from the campus, while the atrium with its tall steel columns is a reference to the antique roots of science.

The programme totalling 12,500 m2 includes not only library facilities, but a cultural centre with a 350-seater auditorium extending from the main body of the building up to a reflecting pool.

Great emphasis is given to provide the interiors with ample daylight, but with due respect for the merciless sun of the arid Lleida region.

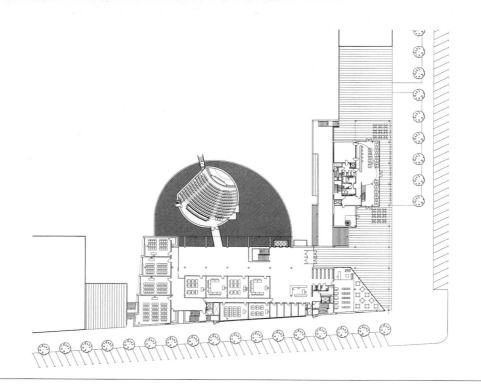

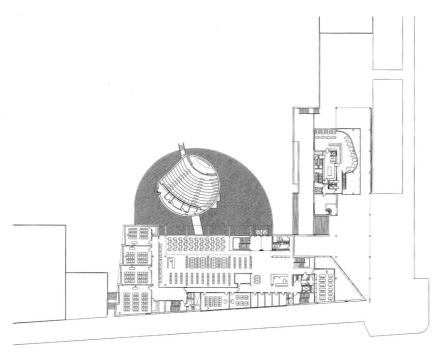

First floor plan.

Ground floor plan.

The narrow gap
separating the auditorium
from the Library block.

North-east model
elevation,
with the lamellar facade
screening off
the Library spaces.

North-east elevation.

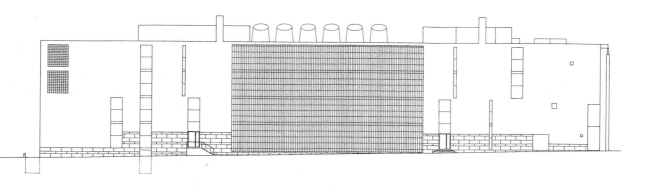

North-west model
elevation,
with the full-height portico
connecting through
to the courtyard space.

North-west elevation.

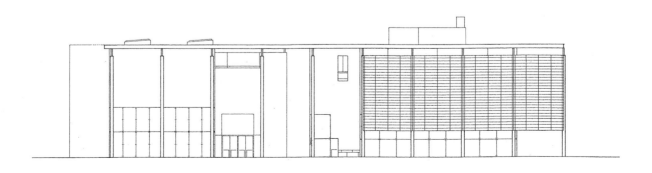

Commerce

Most architects know how difficult it is to combine one's own architectural ideas with trade requisites, but there are only a few that show a real interest in the quandary, and who have achieved in their work a balance between the two extremes. When does the facade of a shopping centre stop being architecture to become publicity? Can a shopping centre become a meeting point for people, for other reasons than consumption? Indeed, can building and merchandise be complementary?

In the heart of Helsinki, the Stockmann Department store have won a prestigious corner facade; here Gullichsen, Kairamo and Vormala designed together a building nearly entirely in glass blocks, that responds by subtraction to the visual stimuli of the city, and that itself becomes an emblem capable of changing skins at different hours of the day and seasons of the year: opaque, semi-transparent, translucid, minimalist yet sensual. The narrow corner, treated like a foreshortened constructivist sculpture, contains besides the entrance, the sign of a flagmast, and leaves no doubt about the possibility of still believing in total art.

In the Shopping centre of Itäkeskus, a satellite city of the capital, the issues to be dealt with were different. The large scale forced the architects to make choices that would be legible from afar: a vertical tower for offices balances the horizontality of the parking block and the shopping centre.

The shopping arcade on the first floor is not laid out like a snare upsetting our sense of direction, but is a public space that belongs to a sequence of places, some of which are exterior. Here a connection with local markets of the past is openly claimed; the pedestrian has a retort to the despotism of automobiles.

The commentary is again different at Veho Auto-City, a fortress dedicated to four-wheels, unfortunately only a small part of which has been built. Here, on the inner side of a large suburban block, architecture gracefully welcomes the automobiles, without considering them vulgar fetishes; rather than shop-windows, they are given three-dimensional pavilions. The slowness of the eye can, for a moment, replace the speed of driving.

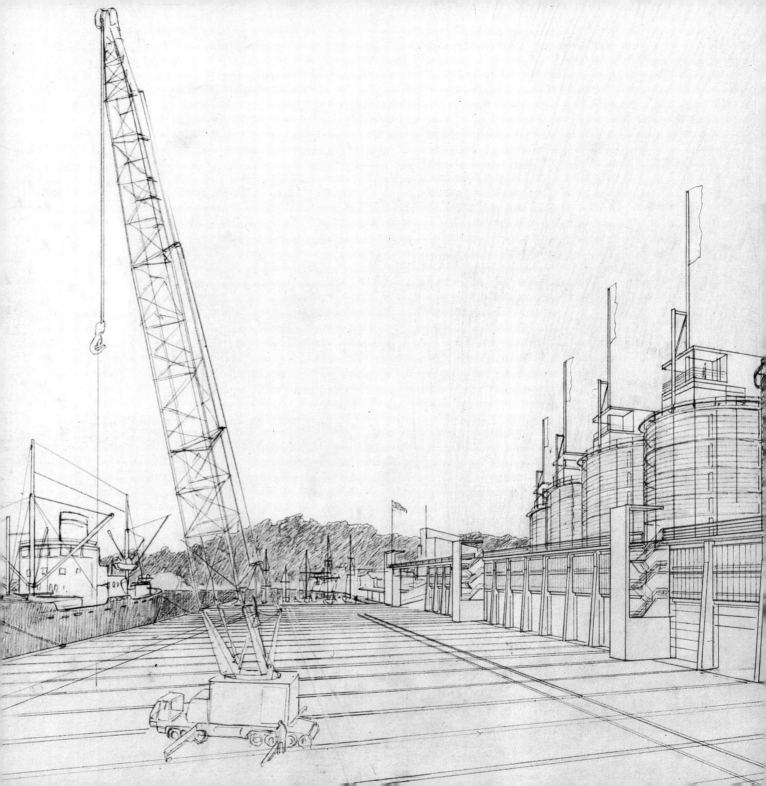

Erkki Kairamo

Itäkeskus Shopping centre
and Office tower
Helsinki, 1987

On the previous two
pages: Office complex,
Naantali. Perspective.

Site plan, showing
the Shopping centre
and the Office tower
on opposite sides
of the railway line.

Itäkeskus is the commercial and cultural centre of
Eastern Helsinki's large suburban area embracing
some 30,000 people.

The task was to design a Shopping centre
over the metro tracks, and an Office tower at the
focal point of the main pedestrian axes to act as a
landmark for the centre.

The Shopping centre complex is not so mu-
ch a discrete building as a vital and integral part of
the area's structure. It is strongly influenced by the
tightly constrained site, an area strictly delimited
by the feeder-bus station, motorway and railtracks
below, and a raised pedestrian square above.

The main motif of the exterior elevation facing the motorway is an illuminated horizontal
glass lantern, which at night appears in the townscape as the horizontal component in the supre-

matist cross composition in which the tower's 82
m-high stairway forms the vertical.

The architecture reflects the vitality of the
place and is designed to take advantage of the i-
nevitable advertisement hoardings and signs as
compositional elements.

The architectural aim of the Office tower
was to produce as slim a building as possible
within the inevitable limitations of an office building containing only sixteen rentable floors.

As well as acting as the vertical in the cross
of light, the tall stairway, which reaches beyond
the extent of the building, adds to the verticality of
the composition. For this reason the ventilation
ducts are also placed on the outside, and both
help to maintain the slenderness of the Tower by
reducing the dimensions of the internal core.

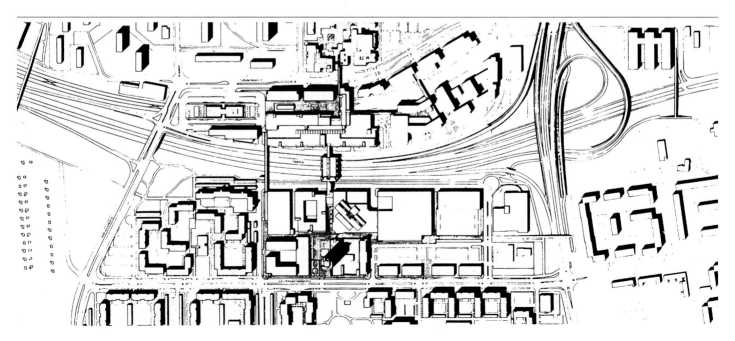

The principal entrance
of the shopping centre,
overlooking
the raised piazza.

First-floor plan,
showing the pedestrian
connection
from the railway station,
through the Shopping
centre, to the raised
piazza.

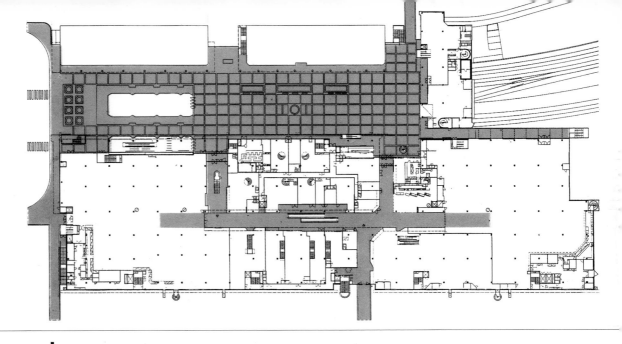

Longitudinal elevation
of the Shopping centre.

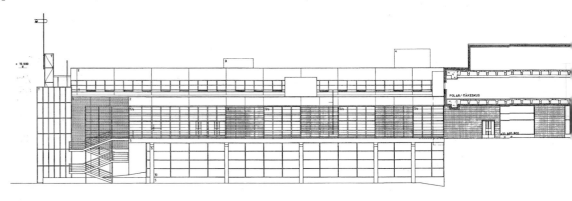

Longitudinal section
through the pedestrian
piazza

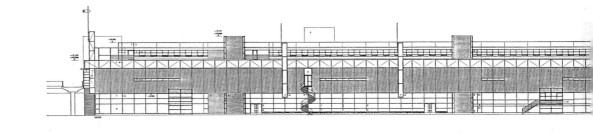

Ground floor plan.

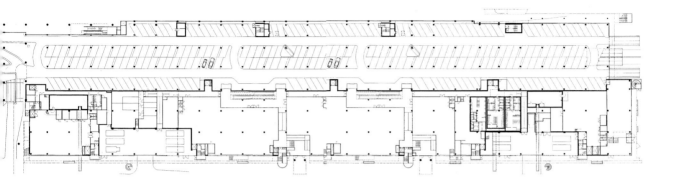

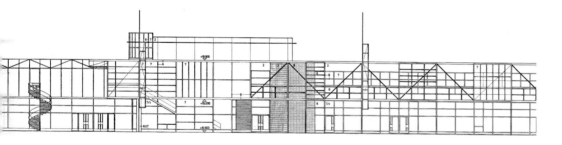

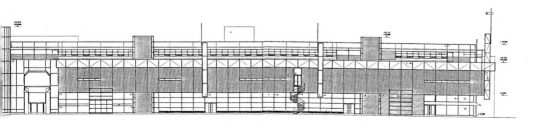

145

Exterior day and night
of the Shopping centre.

The commercial gallery
within the Shopping
centre: cross-section,
view, and perspective
drawing.

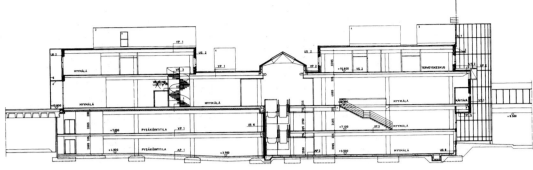

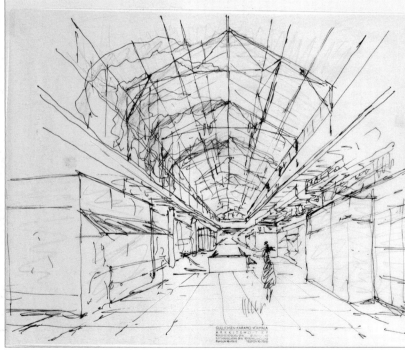

The Office tower seen
from the railway station.

The Office tower
seen from below.

Ground floor plan of the
Office tower.
Note the external ducts.

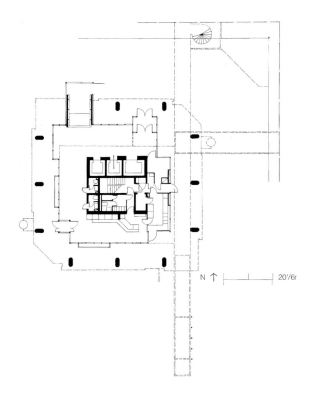

N ↑ | | 20'/6r

Metal carpentry
details and expressive
service ducts
on the Office tower
rooftop.

Kristian Gullichsen
Erkki Kairamo
Timo Vormala

Stockmann's Department store extension Helsinki, 1989

Ground floor plan.

Elevation of Keskuskatu.

View showing
the relationship
to Sigurd Frosterus'
building on the right.

The extension of the big Department store situated on a focal point in the city centre occupies a narrow corner plot surrounded by distinguished neighbours: the old store (Sigurd Frosterus, 1930) and a fragment of a neo-renaissance chateau now integrated in the store (Johan Settergren, 1889).

Three prominent buildings face the new structure across the street: an office building by Eliel Saarinen (1920) and two buildings by Alvar Aalto (1955 and 1969).

Several schemes for the extension were presented over the years. After Frosterus, who produced a number of versions ranging from his proposal submitted in 1924 to the last version in 1956, Alvar Aalto proposed two alternatives, one in 1961 and another in 1966. Notably, all these schemes involved demolition of the neo-renaissance corner.

The new building is the result of an open design competition held in 1984.

The main challenge in filling the missing corner was how to relate the new piece both to the powerful Berlin-inspired, neo-classicist old store and the decorative late renaissance pastiche of a chateau.

The vocabulary of the finished extension echoes the old store, updated in glass and steel.

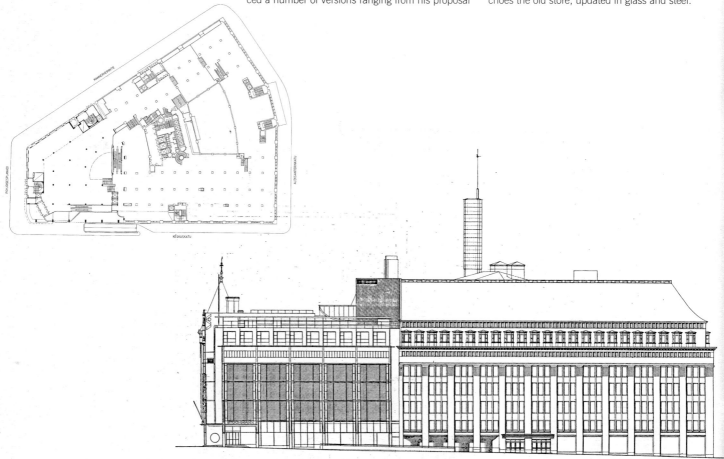

Corner view, showing
the relationship
to the neo-renaissance
chateau on the left.

Corner elevation.

Night view,
with the translucent
glass blocks.

Plan and view
of the stone-clad column.

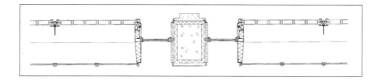

The interior light well.

Erkki Kairamo

Veho Auto-City
Espoo, 1991

Site plan.

Exterior elevation.

This complex, a centre of operations for the country's largest foreign car importer, is aptly situated in a development area at the junction of an urban motorway and the main motor route to the west of Finland. The design makes use of the dynamic surroundings by aiming one of its long facades at the cars rushing by on one motorway, and the other, more relaxed showroom elevation to the other.

The machine idea is very strong in this design. All the mechanical areas — stores, workshops, maintenance and body shops — line up along the edge of the motorway, a tower halts the process, and the whole machine turns at the corner, reappearing as airy showrooms. Thus the L-shaped mass forms a courtyard for the parking of new models.

The architecture, stretching tiled pre-fab concrete elements streamlined with narrow strip windows and deep canopies, and regular loading-bay units, naturally functionalist, is soaked in the aura of speeding motor vehicles.

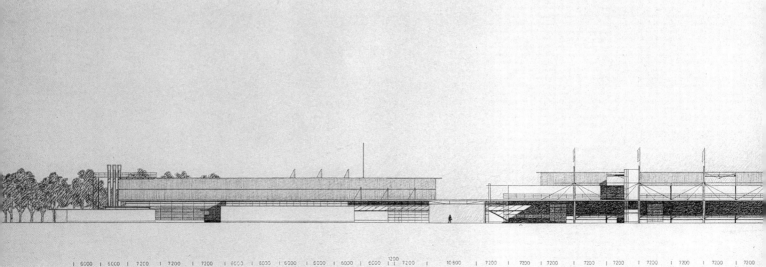

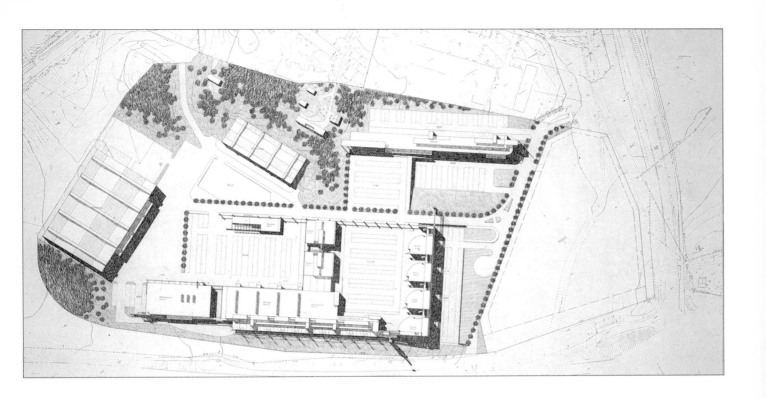

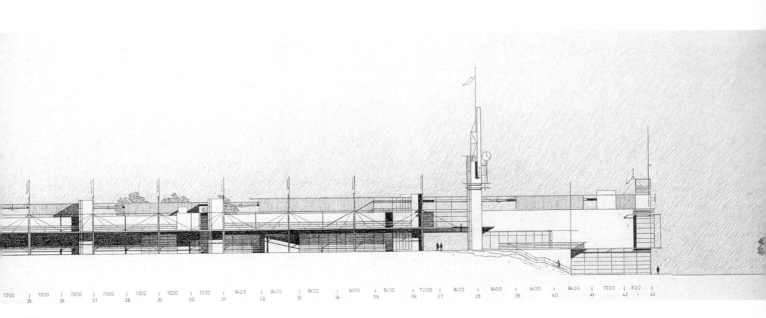

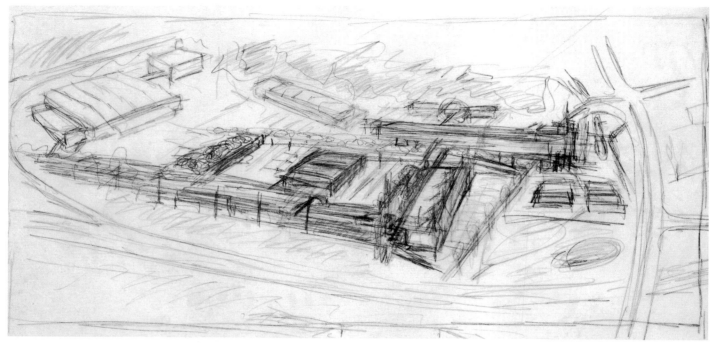

Preliminary sketches.

Final perspectives.

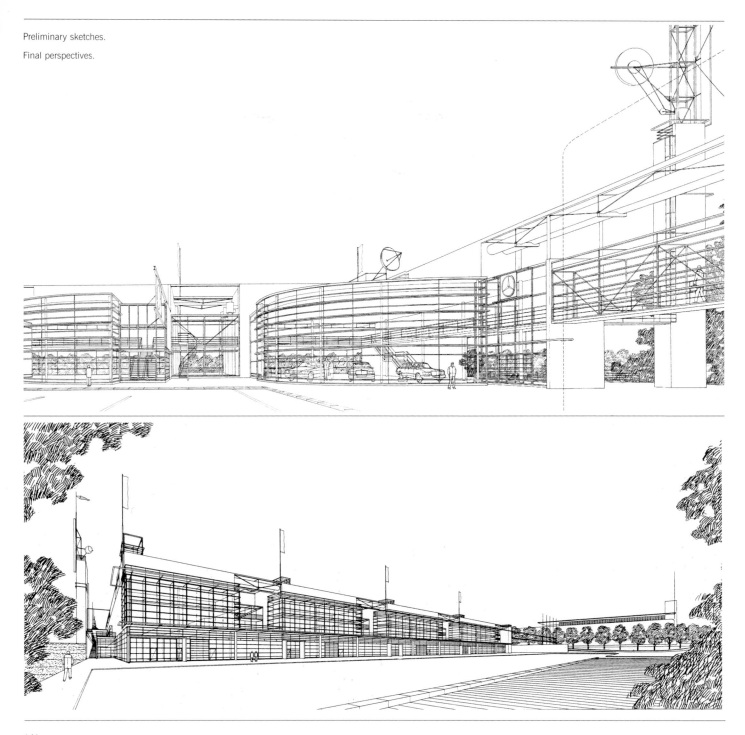

Interior and exterior
elevations.

What has been built
of the project,
showing a strong
horizontality
and the combination
of different materials.

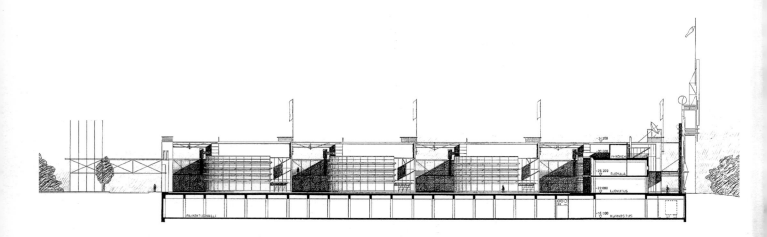

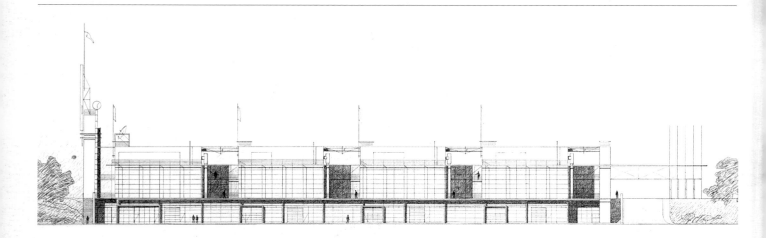

162

Appendix

compiled by Antti Tokola

List of major works

Kristian Gullichsen, Erkki Kairamo and Timo Vormala: 1962–1972. Gullichsen Kairamo Vormala Architects: 1973–1994. Gullichsen Vormala Architects: 1995–

* = built works

1962–1963*
Power plant, Varkaus.
K. Gullichsen, K. Ormio,
L. Kojo.

1963*
Town plan for Vaasa
old town. First prize
in design competition
1963. E. Kairamo,
E. Juutilainen.

1963–1964*
Private house 'Villa
Berner', Pori.
K. Gullichsen.

1964
Plan for Tapiola Town
centre, Espoo. E.
Kairamo, E. Juutilainen,
K. Mikkola, J. Pallasmaa.

1965–1966*
Private house 'Villa
Seppä', Laajasalo, Espoo.
K. Gullichsen.

1966*
Private house 'Villa
Andersson', Sipoo.
K. Gullichsen.

1966*
Private house 'Villa
Drejer', Sipoo.
K. Gullichsen.

1967
Parish centre, Lahti,
project. First prize in
design competition 1967.
K. Gullichsen.

1967*
Extension to Glass factory,
Kuitulasi Oy, Karhula,
K. Gullichsen.

1967–1968*
Power plant,
Hyrylä garrison.
E. Kairamo,
J. Pankakoski.

1967–1970*
Group of dwellings,
Hanikka, Espoo. Two
buildings realized.
E. Kairamo.

1968-1969*
Alvar Aalto exhibition,
Helsinki 1968, Stockholm
1969. K. Gullichsen,
S. Savander.

1968–1970*
Row house, Westend,
Espoo. E. Kairamo,
A. Jylhä.

1968–1970*
Central administation
building, Espoo. E.
Kairamo, E. Juutilainen,
K. Mikkola, J. Pallasmaa.

1968–1973*
Moduli building system.
K. Gullichsen,
J. Pallasmaa.

1970*
Office building,
Gyldenintie, Helsinki.
K. Gullichsen, P. Piha,
L. Kojo.

1971
Student building,
Helsinki, project, first
prize in design
competition 1971.
T. Vormala, I. Aarniala,
J. Koskinen.

1971
Church, Kouvola. First
prize in design
competition 1971.
T. Vormala, I. Aarniala,
J. Koskinen.

1971–1973
Restoration and
development plan for
Suomenlinna Fortress,
Helsinki. First prize in

design competition 1971.
Amended plan 1973.
E. Kairamo, R. Lahtinen.

1972*
Private house 'La Petite
Maison', Grasse, France.
K. Gullichsen.

1972–1979*
Textile factory,
Marimekko Oy, Helsinki.
E. Kairamo, R. Lahtinen,
T. Vormala, P. Hokkanen,
A. Jylhä.

1974–1982
Arts centre, Pasila,
Helsinki, project.
K. Gullichsen, T. Vormala,
L. Kojo.

1975–1977*
Paper mill, A. Ahlström
Oy, Varkaus. E. Kairamo,
T. Vormala, P. Piha,
J. Sutela, P. Ojamies,
A. Jylhä.

1976–1980*
Art gallery, Pori.
Alteration to listed
bonded warehouse by G.
Nyström. K. Gullichsen,
K. Ormio, J. Sutela,
A. Jylhä.

1977
Residential block,
Kuitinmäki, Espoo.
First prize in design
competition 1977.
K. Gullichsen, T. Vormala.

1977–1978*
Kindergarten,
Noormarkku.
K. Gullichsen, A. Jylhä,
J. Sutela, P. Ojamies.

1977–1979*
Housing area, Suutarila,
Helsinki. K. Gullichsen,
T. Vormala, P. Ojamies,

C. Schalin,
M. Lapinleimu.

1977–1979*
Residential block,
Tikkurila, Vantaa. E.
Kairamo, A. Jylhä.

1977–1981*
Malmi church, Helsinki.
First prize in design
competition 1977,
completion 1980–1981.
K. Gullichsen, L. Kojo,
M. Linko, A. Jylhä.

1978
Forum block, Helsinki.
Second prize in design
competition. K.
Gullichsen, E. Kairamo, T.
Vormala, K. Koskinen.

1978
Marina, Suomenlinna,
Helsinki. E. Kairamo,
K. Koskinen.

1978–1984
Länsi-Mustasaari Area
plan, Suomenlinna,
Helsinki. E. Kairamo,
K. Koskinen.

1978–1987*
'Landmark' Office
building, Itäkeskus,
Helsinki. First prize in
design competition 1978,
completion 1984–1987.
E. Kairamo, T. Vormala,
H. Mäkinen, A. Jylhä,
P. Ojamies, C. Schalin,
J. Sutela.

1979
Office building, Kallio,
Helsinki, project.
E. Kairamo, A. Jylhä,
K. Koskinen.

1979–1980*
Housing. Vitsaskuja,
Konala, Helsinki. T.

Vormala, M. Lapinleimu.

1979–1981*
Residential blocks
Linnankatu 11 and
Katajanokanranta 1,
Helsinki. K. Gullichsen,
T. Koivu, M. Salo.

1979–1983*
Kauniainen Church.
First prize in design
competition 1979,
completed 1983. K.
Gullichsen, T. Vormala,
M. Linko, A. Jylhä,
H. Nieminen.

1980*
Extension to Paper mill,
Joutseno Pulp Oy, Lohja.
E. Kairamo, J. Sutela,
M. Nylen, A. Jylhä.

1980*
Housing. Heinäkuja,
Varisto, Vantaa.
T. Vormala, P. Ojamies,
C. Schalin.

1980–1982*
Metropolitan area
information centre,
Itäkeskus, Helsinki.
T. Vormala, R. Jallinoja,
M-V. Salo, T. Koivu.

1980–1989*
Näkinpuisto Residential
area, Helsinki. First prize
in design competition
1980, completed 1989.
T. Vormala, R. Jallinoja,
J. Sutela, T. Saarelainen,
M. Nylen.

1981–1983*
Kukkaskartanon Day-care
centre, Katajanokka,
Helsinki. T. Vormala,
M-V. Salo, T. Koivu.

1981–1984*
Shopping centre,

Itäkeskus, Helsinki.
E. Kairamo, H. Mäkinen,
K. Koskinen.
M. Kajosaari, T.
Saarelainen, E. Kilpiö,
J. Linko, M. Pesonen,
K. Friman, A. Jylhä.

1982*
Housing. Liinasaarenkuja,
Westend, Espoo.
E. Kairamo, J. Maunula,
A. Jylhä, C. Schalin,
M. Nylen.

1982–1985*
Residential block.
Puustellinpolku,
Malminkartano, Helsinki.
T. Vormala, J. Sutela,
M-V. Salo, T. Koivu.

1982–1989*
Cultural centre 'Poleeni',
Pieksämäki. First prize in
design competition 1982,
construction 1988–1989.
K. Gullichsen, T. Vormala,
A. Jylhä, M. Linko,
E. Kilpiö, K. Friman,
A. Korjula.

1982–1995*
Residential area,
Kivenlahti, Espoo.
Construction in six phases
from 1982–1995.
T. Vormala, E. Kilpiö, M.
Kakkonen, J. Ylä-Outinen,
M-V. Salo.

1983
Residential block,
Hiiralankaari, Westend,
Espoo. E. Kairamo,
J. Maunula, T. Kauppinen,
P. Nieminen, M. Nylen,
A. Jylhä.

1983–1985
Housing, Pisanniitty,
Olari, Espoo,
project.
T. Vormala, M. Linko,

J. Linko.

1983–1985*
Housing block. Toiskantie,
Malminkartano, Helsinki.
T. Vormala, J. Linko.

1983–1985*
Housing.
Kyläsuutarinpuisto,
Suutarila, Helsinki. T.
Vormala, M. Lapinleimu.

1983–1988*
Savings Bank,
Lappeenranta. First prize
in design competition
1983, completion
1987–1988. K. Gullichsen,
T. Vormala, M. Kajosaari,
E. Kilpiö.

1984
Official Residence of the
President of Finland,
Helsinki, project.
Purchase in design
competition 1984. K.
Gullichsen, T. Vormala,
M. Nylen, M. Linko,
A. Korjula, P. Bulow.

1984–1990*
Vaakuna Hotel, Kokkola.
First prize in design
competition 1984.
Alteration and extension
of listed electrical
company building by S.
Frosterus and G. Strengell
as a bank building.
T. Vormala,
J. Haukkavaara, J. Linko.

1984–1989*
Extension to Stockmann
Department store,
Helsinki. First prize in
design competition 1984,
completed 1989.
K. Gullichsen,
E. Kairamo, T. Vormala,
J. Sutela, M.Muoniovaara,
M. Kajosaari, J. Linko,

J. Haukkavaara, E.
Jokiniemi, T. Saarelainen,
T. Patomo, V. Huttunen,
N. Davies, E. Kilpiö,
A. Jylhä, A. Korjula,
P. Bulow.

1985*
Additive treatment plant
for Paper mill, A.
Ahlström Oy, Varkaus. E.
Kairamo, J. Haukkavaara,
T. Kauppinen.

1985–1991*
Fire station, Niittykumpu,
Espoo. E. Kairamo,
T. Saarelainen, T. Patomo,
N. Davies, J. Murole,
A. Jylhä.

1986
Bank of Finland, Turku,
project, third prize in
design competition 1986.
E. Kairamo, T. Vormala.

1986
Central administration
area, Mansikkala, project,
Second prize in design
competition 1986.
E. Kairamo, T. Vormala,
A. Jylhä, T. Saarelainen.

1986–1990*
Housing and offices,
Ylämalmintori, Helsinki.
T. Vormala, M. Linko,
S. Pyyhtiä.

1986–1997*
Summer residence 'Villa
Aulikki', Halskär.
E. Kairamo.

1987
Commercial centre, Pori,
project. Entry in design
competition 1987.
K. Gullichsen, T. Vormala.

1987
Gaselli block, Helsinki,

project. First prize in
design competition 1987.
K. Gullichsen,
T. Vormala, H. Mäkinen,
J. Haukkavaara.

1987–1990*
Government offices,
Joensuu. T. Vormala,
H. Mäkinen, M. Pesonen,
A. Jylhä, K. Hannunkari,
L. Maaranen.

1987–1991*
Car showrooms and Sales
complex, Veho Auto-City,
Espoo. First prize in
design competition 1987,
first phase completion
1988–1991. E. Kairamo,
T. Vormala,
T. Saarelainen, E.
Jokiniemi, V. Huttunen,
S. Pyyhtiä, S. Raitanen,
N. Davies, A. Jylhä.

1987–1992*
Grand Marina Hotel,
Katajanokka, Helsinki.
Alteration to listed
warehouse building
by L. Sonck and S. A.
Lindqvist. T. Vormala,
M. Kajosaari,
L. Maaranen, J. Linko.

1988
Residence of Finnish
Ambassador, Geneva,
Switzerland, project.
K. Gullichsen.

1988
Kameeli block, Helsinki,
project. Entry in design
competition 1988. K.
Gullichsen, H. Mäkinen.

1988–1990*
Solid fuel power station
K6, Enso-Gutzeit Oy,
Varkaus. E. Kairamo,
H. Mäkinen, T.
Saarelainen, T. Patomo,

A. Jylhä, L. Maaranen,
E. Davidsdottir.

1988–1992
Centre for Radiation
Safety, Kerava, project.
T. Vormala, J. Sutela,
A. Jylhä.

1988–1993*
Residential block
in housing fair 'Expo
Wohnen 2000', Stuttgart,
Germany. K. Gullichsen,
M. Pesonen.

1989
Office building
'Saharannan
merimaisematilat',
Naantali, project. First
prize in design
competition 1989.
T. Vormala, E. Kairamo,
H. Mäkinen.

1989
Church and Parish
centre, Pirkkala, project.
Entry in design
competition 1989.
K. Gullichsen,
J. Haukkavaara.

1989
Finlayson area, Tampere,
project. Entry in design
competition 1989.
T. Vormala, J. Linko,
M. Nylén.

1989–1990*
Semi-detached private
houses. Lyökkiniemi,
Westend, Espoo.
E. Kairamo, A. Jylhä,
V. Huttunen.

1990
Bridge, Kärkistensalmi,
project. First prize in ideas
competition 1990.
E. Kairamo, V. Huttunen,
R. Sormunen. Purchase,
E. Kairamo, M. Ollila.

1990
Housing area. Smista
Park, Huddinge, Sweden.
Project. K. Gullichsen,
J. Haukkavaara.

1990–1997*
Residential area, Lahti
Housing Fair. Shared first
prize in design
competition 1990. One
block constructed 1992,
two in 1995–1997.
T. Vormala, J. Linko,
S. Raitanen.

1991
Moderna Museet
and Arkitekturmuseet,
Stockholm. Sweden.
Project. Purchase in
international design
competition 1991.
K. Gullichsen, T. Vormala,
J. Haukkavaara.

1991
Residential building,
Kauppiaankatu,
Katajanokka. Project.
T. Vormala, H. Mäkinen.

1991
Office building. Piilikuja,
Malmi, Helsinki. Project.
T. Vormala, T. Saarelainen.

1991
Museum of Forestry,
Punkaharju, project.
Entry in design
competition 1991.
T. Vormala, H. Mäkinen.

1991
Commercial building.
Smista Park Allé,
Huddinge, Sweden.
Project. K. Gullichsen,
H. Mäkinen,
J. Haukkavaara.

1991
Offices and Industrial

complex 'Smista
Pentagonen', Huddinge,
Sweden, project.
H. Mäkinen,
J. Haukkavaara.

1991
Residential area,
Wilhelminapark, Breda,
Holland. Project. K.
Gullichsen, H. Mäkinen.

1991–1995*
Residential area.
Käpyläntie, Käpylä,
Helsinki. T. Vormala,
T. Saarelainen.

1991–1998*
Residential block
'Linnanrakentajanpuisto',
Helsinki. T. Vormala,
J. Sutela.

1992
Aleksi 2002 Plan,
Helsinki. K. Gullichsen,
H. Mäkinen.

1992
Main library, Espoo,
Three designs:
second prize in design
competition 1992:
K. Gullichsen,
J. Haukkavaara.
Second prize: E. Kairamo,
A. Jylhä, V. Huttunen.
Purchase: T. Vormala,
T. Pessi.

1992
Residential block,
Veräjämäki, Helsinki,
project first prize
in design competition
1992.
T. Vormala, E. Kilpiö.

1992
Theatre Institute,
Helsinki, project.
K. Gullichsen,
J. Haukkavaara.

1992
Residential block, Steel
and Glass Workshop,
Jansen/Vegla, Project.
K. Gullichsen,
J. Haukkavaara.

1992
Recreational centre,
Mustikkamaa, Helsinki,
project. T. Vormala,
J. Haukkavaara.

1992
Residential block
'Olympia', Vaasa, project.
Entry in design
competition 1992.
K. Gullichsen, J.
Haukkavaara, J. Linko.

1992
Office building,
Sörnäisten rantatie,
Helsinki, project.
T. Vormala, T. Saarelainen.

1992–1993*
Land use plan,
Munkinmäki,
Kirkkonummi.
First prize in design
competition 1992.
E. Kairamo,
V. Huttunen, A. Jylhä,
T. Saarelainen, J. Sinkkilä.

1992–1995*
Residential block.
Itämerenkatu, Ruoholahti,
Helsinki. T. Vormala,
J. Sutela, T. Saarelainen.

1992–1995*
Residential block.
Linnanrakentajankulma,
Herttoniemi, Helsinki.
T. Vormala, S. Raitanen.

1992–1995*
Geodetic Institute,
Masala, Kirkkonummi.
T. Vormala, M. Pesonen,
A. Jylhä, A. Jaaksi.

1993
Residential block in
Housing Fair, Pietarsaari,
project. Entry in design
competition 1993.
T. Vormala, J. Linko,
J. Sutela.

1993
Töölönlahti Feasibility
study and preliminary
designs, Helsinki.
T. Vormala, H. Mäkinen.

1993*
Boathouse, Espoo.
E. Kairamo.

1993–1995*
Residential building
'Myllytien Olympos',
Helsinki. First prize in
design competition 1993,
completion 1994–1995.
K. Gullichsen, J. Sutela,
J. Haukkavaara.

1993–1995*
Private house 'Villa
Haltia', Kangasala.
K. Gullichsen,
J. Haukkavaara.

1993–1998*
Micro-electronic research
centre, VTT electronics,
Otaniemi, Espoo.
T. Vormala, H. Mäkinen,
A. Jylhä, M. Pesonen,
A. Jaaksi, N. Davies.

1993–*
Embassy of Finland,
Stockholm, Sweden.
K. Gullichsen,
J. Haukkavaara, A. Jylhä.
Under construction.

1993–
Residential area,
Artilleripark, Arnheim,
The Netherlands, project.
K. Gullichsen, E. Kilpiö,
J. Haukkavaara.

1994–1995*
Residential block
'Helsingin Fokka',
Ruoholahti, Helsinki.
T. Vormala, S. Raitanen.

1994–1995*
Residential block
'Helsingin Spinnu',
Ruoholahti, Helsinki.
T. Vormala,
T. Saarelainen.

1994–1995*
School of Economics,
Vallila, Helsinki.
Alteration and
refurbishment.
T. Vormala, E. Kilpiö,
A. Jylhä.

1994–1996*
Housing area.
Köökarinkuja, Laajasalo,
Helsinki. T. Vormala,
J. Linko, S. Raitanen.

1994–1997*
Residential area
'Lauttasaaren Meritähti',
Helsinki. T. Vormala,
S. Raitanen, J. Linko.

1994–1999*
Commercial building
'Ruoholahden Metrotori',
Helsinki. First phase
1994–1995, second stage
1997–1999. T. Vormala,
E. Jokiniemi, H. Mäkinen,
A. Jylhä.

1995
Bus terminal area,
Kamppi, Helsinki.
Preliminary designs.
T. Vormala, H. Mäkinen.

1995
Britannia House, Brussels,
Belgium. Renovation
and alteration, project.
K. Gullichsen, H.
Mäkinen, J. Haukkavaara.

1995
Area of residential and
office buildings, Norrtull,
Stockholm, Sweden.
Project. K. Gullichsen,
J. Haukkavaara.

1995–1998*
Residential block
'Herttoniemenhuippu',
Sorsavuorenkatu,
Helsinki. T. Vormala,
J. Sutela.

1995–1998*
Community facility and
columbarium, Kauniainen
church. K. Gullichsen,
E. Kilpiö, A. Jylhä.

1995–1998*
Residential block,
Laivalahdenportti,
Helsinki. T. Vormala,
M. Lapinleimu, A. Jylhä.

1995–1998*
Residential block,
Linnanrakentajanpuisto,
Helsinki. T. Vormala,
J. Sutela.

1995–1998*
Residential area,
Tikkurilan Veturipiha,
Vantaa. T. Vormala,
T. Saarelainen.

1995–1998*
Residential area.
Valtimontie, Kumpula,
Helsinki. T. Vormala,
T. Saarelainen.

1996–*
Residential block,
Vuosaari, Helsinki.
First prize in design
competition. 1996.
T. Vormala, S. Raitanen.
Under construction.

1996–
University library, Lleida,

Biographies

Spain. First stage of design competition 1996, second stage 1997, first prize, project. K. Gullichsen.

1996–1997*
Kalastajatorppa Hotel renovation and alteration, Helsinki. T. Vormala, H. Mäkinen.

1996–1997*
Residential block, Paciuksenkaari, Helsinki. T. Vormala, M. Lapinleimu.

1996–1998*
Office building 'Allergiatalo', Pikku-Huopalahti, Helsinki. T. Vormala, E. Kilpiö, A. Jylhä, M. Pesonen.

1996–1998*
Residential block, Laivalahdenkaari, Helsinki. T. Vormala, M. Lapinleimu.

1997
Residential block, SOK area, Jollas, preliminary design. T. Vormala, J. Sutela.

1997
Residential block 'Katrinpuisto', Helsinki, project. T. Vormala, T. Saarelainen.

1997
Area plan. Aurinkolahti, Vuosaari, Helsinki, project. First prize in design competition 1997. T. Vormala, J. Linko.

1997–1998*
Extension and alteration to Art Gallery, Pori. K. Gullichsen, J. Haukkavaara.

1997–1999*
Residential block 'Merikannonranta', Helsinki. T. Vormala, S. Raitanen, J. Linko.

1997–*
Residential block 'Merikannonpuisto', Helsinki. T. Vormala, S. Raitanen, J. Linko. Under construction.

1997–*
Residential block 'Kesäillanvalssi', Helsinki. T. Vormala, S. Raitanen. Under construction.

1997-*
Residential block 'Dockside', Helsinki. T. Vormala, E. Kilpiö, S. Raitanen. Under construction.

1997–*
Residential block 'Luoteistähti', Helsinki. T. Vormala, M. Pesonen. Under construction.

1997–*
Medical research centre Biomedicum, Helsinki. First prize in design competition 1997. T. Vormala, M. Lummaa, E. Karonen, V. Karonen, M. Lapinleimu. Under construction.

1999–
Residential area, Saltsjöbaden, Nacka, Sweden, project. K. Gullichsen, J. Haukkavaara, K. Lybeck.

Kristian Gullichsen was born in Helsinki in 1932. In 1939 he moved into Villa Mairea, by Alvar and Aino Aalto. In 1951 he entered the Helsinki University of Technology (where, he confesses, he learned to cheat and how to drink beer); he graduated in 1960. In between his academic studies, he held the position as errand boy in Alvar Aalto's studio, being responsible for sharpening the pencils. He also worked for Toivo Kurhonen and Heikki Siren. Between 1961 and 1973 he held his own office, and collaborated with Juhani Pallasmaa. In 1973 he formed the partnership with Erkki Kairamo and Timo Vormala. At present he is Chairman of the Alvar Aalto Foundation and of the Finnish Museum of Architecture.

Erkki Kairamo was born in Helsinki in 1936. During his studies at the Helsinki University of Technology, he worked in the offices of Osmo Sipari, Osmo Lappo and others; he graduated in 1963. Until 1973 he collaborated with Erkki Juutilainen, Kirmo Mikkola, Juhani Pallasmaa and Reijo Lahtinen. In 1973 he formed the partnership with Kristian Gullichsen and Timo Vormala. Among the awards he won: the 1978 Finnish State Award for Architecture, and the 1984 Annual Steel Construction Award. He died in 1994.

Timo Vormala was born in Merikarvia. in 1942. He graduated in 1971 from the Helsinki University of Technology. In 1973 he formed the partnership with Kristian Gullichsen and Erkki Kairamo. In 1999 he won the award for the Construction Project of the Year.

List of associates
1973–99

Gullichsen Kairamo Vormala Architects and Gullichsen Vormala Architects

Markus Aaltonen
Leena Arola
Johanna Arjosaari
Vijay Arya
Tuula Asikainen
Meike Berking
Severi Blomstedt
Petteri Bülow
Senja Carlsson
Edda Davidsdóttir
Nikolas Davies
Sami Ekman
Marina Fogdell
Kimmo Friman
Annika Groop
Juho Grönholm
Alvar Gullichsen
Kristian Gullichsen
Olli Hakanen
Kristiina Hannunkari
Jyri Haukkavaara
Marja Heikkilä
Mika Heinonen
Arto Huttunen
Vesa Huttunen
Risto Iivonen
Asmo Jaaksi
Reijo Jallinoja
Sofie Johansson
Erkki Jokiniemi
Eeva Jonkka
Aulikki Jylhä
Kaisa Kainula
Eero Kairamo
Erkki Kairamo
Jaakko Kairamo
Martti Kajosaari
Erkki Karonen
Virpi Karonen
Timo Kauppinen
Eeva Kilpiö
Katja Kinnarinen
Timo Koivu
Lasse Kojo
Jouko Koskinen
Keijo Koskinen
Ahti Korjula
Kristiina Kölhi
Johanna Lahtinen
Kirsi Laitala
Marja Lapinleimu
Kati Lehesmaa
Birgitta Lehtonen
Anneli Linden
Jukka Linko

Matti Linko
Martiina Linna
Kai Lohman
Annika Lummaa
Matti Lummaa
Kajsa Lybeck
Lasse Maaranen
Sigridur Magnúsdóttir
Ulla Mantsinen
Mari Matomäki
Juhani Maunula
Marja Mikkola-Pärnänen
Matti Muoniovaara
Jussi Murole
Heikki Mäkinen
Meri Mäkipentti
Roy Mänttäri
Satu Niemelä
Heikki Nieminen
Pekka Nieminen
Minna Nissi
Maritta Nylén-Linko
Ahto Ollikainen
Outi-Kaisa Ollikainen
Pertti Ojamies
Kalevi Ormio
Juhani Pallasmaa
Erja Palonkoski
Timo Patomo
Sirkku Paulin
Maaret Pesonen
Pentti Piha
Maija Polovtseff-Ponomaref
Sirpa Pyyhtiä
Susanna Raitanen
Eeva Rantala
Bruno Redureau
Eva Rosengren
Markku Ruokonen
Tapio Saarelainen
Mattiveikko Salo
Christel Schalin
Rosemarie Schnitzler
Jyrki Sinkkilä
Sirkka-Liisa Sundvall
Petteri Suominen
Jaakko Sutela
Britt-Maj Svahn
Katriina Teräsvuori
Jari Tirkkonen
Marjo Toivari
Reija Toivio
Antti Tokola
Karoly Toth

Kaisa Tynkkynen
Anna Vaahtera
Taru Wegelius
Dieter Wienkoop
Martin Wolff
Timo Vormala
Casper Wrede
Jani Wuorimaa
Jyrki Ylä-Outinen

Bibliography

Books

Fabrizio I. Apollonio (ed.), *Architettura per lo spazio sacro*, exhibition catalogue, Umberto Allemandi & c., Bologna, 1996.

Francisco Asencio Cerver, *Commercial space: shopping malls*, [Mies], Rotovision, [s.a.] Francisco Asencio Cerver, *New Architecture. 01: a selection of contemporary architecture*, Atrium, Barcelona, 1996.

Hans-J. Becker, Wolfram Schlote, *Neuer Wohnbau in Finnland = New Housing in Finland*, 2. auflage/edition, Karl Krämer Verlag, Stuttgart, 1964.

Pascal Chossegros, Nicolas Borel. *Mediterranean Houses: Côte d'Azur and Provence*, Editorial Gustavo Gili, Barcelona, 1991.

William J. R. Curtis, *Modern Architecture Since 1900*, third revised, expanded and redesigned edition, Phaidon Press Ltd., London, 1996.

Alfredo Devido, *House Design. Art and Practice*, New York, John Wiley and Sons, Inc., 1996.

Kenneth Frampton, *Modern Architecture. A Critical History*, third edition, Thames and Hudson, London, 1992.

Vilhelm Helander, Simo Rista, *Suomalainen rakennustaide = Modern Architecture in Finland*, Kirjayhtymä Oy, Helsinki, 1987.

Helsingin Stockmannin laajennuskilpailu, exhibition catalogue, Suomen rakennustaiteen museo, Helsinki, 1985.

Arvi Ilonen, *Helsinki-Espoo-Kauniainen-Vantaa. Arkkitehtuuriopas = Arkitekturguide = An Architectural Guide*, Otava, Helsinki, 1990.

Martti Jaatinen (ed.), *Suomi rakentaa 3 = Finland bygger 3*, exhibition catalogue, Suomen rakennustaiteen museo, Helsinki, 1963.

Jouni Kaipia, Lauri Putkonen, *Suomen arkkitehtuuriopas = Arkitekturguide till Finland = A Guide to Finnish Architecture*, Otava, Helsinki, 1997.

Jouni Kaipia (ed.), *Tehdään betonista. Betoni suomalaisessa arkkitehtuurissa = Concrete in Finnish Architecture*, exhibition catalogue, Suomen betoniteollisuuden keskusjärjestö ry/ Suomen rakennustaiteen museo, 1989.

Jouni Kaipia, Tim Von Konow (ed.), *Suomi rakentaa 8 = Finland bygger 8*, exhibition catalogue, Suomen rakennustaiteen museo, Helsinki, 1992.

Timo Koho, *Suomalaisen arkkitehtuurin 60-luku. Konstruktivismi ja järjestelmäajattelu*, Rakennustieto Oy, Helsinki, 1994.

Timo Koho, *Alvar Aallon jälkeinen Suomi. Arkkitehtuurin kuva 1976-1987*, Rakennustieto Oy, Helsinki, 1995.

Markku Komonen et al., *Muoto ja rakenne: Konstruktivismi Suomen modernissa arkkitehtuurissa, kuvataiteessa ja taideteollisuudessa*, exhibition catalogue, Ateneumin taidemuseo, Helsinki, 1981.

Maija Kärkkäinen (ed.), *Functionalism: utopia or the way forward?* (5th International Alvar Aalto Symposium, Jyväskylä, 1991). Alvar Aalto Symposium, Jyväskylä, 1992.

Kauko Linna, Risto Pesonen, Eeva Pikkalainen (ed.), *Kivitalo*, Rakennustieto Oy, Helsinki, 1998.

Llibre de les biblioteques imaginàries de la Universitat de Lleida = Libro de las bibliotecas imaginarias de la Universitat de Lleida = The Imaginary Libraries of the Universitat de Lleida, Universitat de Lleida, 1997.

Pirkko-Liisa Louhenjoki-Schulman (ed.), *Synthesis: Architecture, Craftmanship and Design. International conference on architecture, urban planning and design*, Espoo 4.-6.9.1989. SAFA, Helsinki, 1990.

Patrick Mauger, *Centres commerciaux*, Moniteur, Paris, 1991.

Jarmo Maunula (ed.), *Suomi rakentaa 4 = Finland bygger 4*, exhibition catalogue, Suomen rakennustaiteen museo, Helsinki, 1970.

Jarmo Maunula (ed.), *Suomi rakentaa 5 = Finland bygger 5*, exhibition catalogue, Suomen rakennustaiteen museo, Helsinki, 1976.

Dirk Meyhofer, *Contemporary European architects 2*, Taschen, Köln, 1994.

La modernité: Un projet inachevé: 40 architectes, Moniteur, Paris, 1982.

Riitta Myllylä (ed.), *Ten Finnish Libraries = Tio bibliotek i Finland = Katse kymmeneen kirjastoon*, Suomen Kirjastoseura, Helsinki, [s.a.]

Erkki Mäkiö, Lauri Putkonen, Timo Tuomi, *Rautaiset rakenteet: Rauta ja teräs suomalaisessa arkkitehtuurissa*, exhibition catalogue, Suomen rakennustaiteen museo, 1998.

Riitta Nikula, *Rakennettu maisema. Suomen arkkitehtuurin vuosisadat = Architecture and Landscape. The Building of Finland = Bebaute landschaft. Finnlands architektur im uberblick = Construire avec le paysage.*

Le modèle Finlandais = Costruire col paesaggio. L'Architettura Finlandese nei secoli = Construir con el paisage. Breve historia de la Arquitectura Finlandesa, Otava, Helsinki, 1993, 1996.

Christian Norberg-Schultz, Scandinavia - Architettura, gli ultimi vent'anni, Electa, Milan, 1990.

Marja-Riitta Norri (ed.), Suomi rakentaa 6 = Finland bygger 6, exhibition catalogue, Suomen rakennustaiteen museo, Helsinki, 1980.

Marja-Riitta Norri, Virpi Kumpulainen (ed.), Aulikki Jylhä (foreword), Erkki Kairamo - Luonnoksia/Sketches, exhibition catalogue, Suomen rakennustaiteen museo, Helsinki, 1997.

Marja-Riitta Norri, Maija Kärkkäinen (ed.), Arkkitehtuurin nykyhetki: 7 näkökulmaa = An Architectural present: 7 approaches, exhibition catalogue, Suomen rakennustaiteen museo, Helsinki, 1990.

Marja-Riitta Norri, Kristiina Paatero (ed.), Rakennettu puusta = Timber Construction in Finland, exhibition catalogue, Suomen rakennustaiteen museo, Helsinki, 1996.

Ilpo Okkonen, Asko Salokorpi, Suomalainen arkkitehtuuri 1900-luvulla = Finnish Architecture in the 20th Century,

Gummerus, Jyväskylä, 1985.

Pirjo Pennanen-Kaila, Kari Kuosma, Aaro Artto (ed.), Suomalainen pientalo, exhibition catalogue, Suomen rakennustaiteen museo, Helsinki, 1986.

Scott Poole, The New Finnish Architecture, Rizzoli, New York, 1992.

Pere Joan Ravetllat Mira, Block Housing: a contemporary perspective, Editorial Gustavo Gili, Barcelona, 1992.

Asko Salokorpi, Suomen arkkitehtuuri 1900-luvulla = Finsk Arkitektur = Modern Architecture in Finland = Finnische Architektur, Kustannusosakeyhtiö Tammi, Helsinki, 1970; Wahlström & Widstrand, 1970; Praeger Publishers, Inc., New York, 1970; Verlag Ullstein GmbH, Frankfurt/M-Berlin-Wien, 1970.

H. C. Schulitz, Industriearchitektur in Europa = Industrial architecture in Europe, Ernst & Sohn Verlag, Berlin, 1992.

Ignasi De Solá-Morales, Xavier Costa (ed.), Present and futures: architecture in cities, Collegi d'Arquitectes de Catalunya, Barcelona, 1996.

Colin St. John Wilson (intr.), Gullichsen/Kairamo/ Vormala, Editorial

Gustavo Gili, Barcelona, 1994.

Pekka Suhonen,Uutta suomalaista arkkitehtuuria = Ny arkitektur i Finland = Neue architektur in Finnland, Kustannusosakeyhtiö Tammi, Helsinki, 1967.

Kaarin Taipale (ed.), Suomi rakentaa 7 = Finland bygger 7, exhibition catalogue, Suomen rakennustaiteen museo, Helsinki, 1986.

Egon Tempel, Suomalaista rakennustaidetta tänään = Finsk byggnadskonst i dag, Otava, Helsinki, 1968.

Sanna Vauhkonen (ed.), Suomi rakentaa 9 = Finland bygger 9, exhibition catalogue, Suomen rakennustaiteen museo, Helsinki, 1998.

Journals

A + U, 209/1988.
Abitare, 101/1971, 135/1975, 210/1982, 216/1983.
AIT, 1-2/1994.
AJ, 27/1980.
Archis, 1/1991.
Architect, 12/1997.
de Architect, 12/1987.
Architectural Design, 12/1979.
The Architectural Review, 937/1975, 1117/1990.
Architecture, 9/1989, 9/1993.
Architecture in Greece, 18/1984.
L'architecture d'aujourd'hui, 199/1978, 270/1990, 274/1991.
Architecture Today, 13/1990, 18/1991, 32/1992, 76/1997,

79/1997.
Der Architekt, 4/1987, 1/1995.
Architektur Wettbewerbe, 85/1976, 98/1979, 99/1979, 115/1983, 148/1991, 167/1996, 171/1997.
Architektura CSR, 9-10/1976.
L'Architettura, 407/1989.
Arkitekten, 17/1964, 2/1991.
Arkitektnytt, 20/1982.
Arkitektur, 5/1982.
Arkitektur DK, 3/1985.
Arkitekturtävlingar, 11/1991.
Arkkitehti, 4/1963, 4-5/1964, 7-8/1964, 4/1965, 12/1965, 7-8 1966, 1-2 /1967, 5/1969, 7-8/1972, 2/1973, 4/1973, 8/1973, 2/1975, 5-6/1975, 2/1976, 6/1977, 7/1977, 4/1978, 2/1979, 2/1980, 3/1980, 5-6/1980, 1/1981, 3/1981, 6-7/1981, 1/1982, 4-5/1982, 6/1982, 8/1982, 4/1983, 8/1983, 6/1984, 7/1984, 3/1985, 6-7/1985, 8/1985, 1/1986, 3/1987, 6/1987, 3/1988, 5-6/1989, 8/1989, 1/1990, 2/1990, 3-4/1990, 7-8 1993, 1/1994, 4/1994, 2-3/1996, 5-6/1997, 3/1998.
Arkkitehtiuutiset, 2/1977, 9/1977, 10/1978, 15/1983.
Arquitectura viva, 30/1993, 55/1997.
AV monografias, 55/1995.
Baumeister, 9/1966, 2/1982, 1/1984, 5/1985, 5/1989, 10/1989, 1/1992, 6/1992, 6/1993, 1/1995, 9/1998.
Bauwelt, 46/1991.
Betoni, 1/1997, 3/1997, 3/1998.
Betonituote, 2/1983, 1/1984, 2/1984, 2/1986, 3/1986.
Byggekunst, 2/1976,

7/1986.
Casabella, 540/1987, 562/1989, 573/1990, 599/1983, 630-631/1996.
Casas Internacional, 47/1997.
Costruire in Laterizio, 22/1991.
Detail, 6/1982, 3/1993, 2/1994.
Deutsche Bauzeitung, 5/1981.
Domus, 508/1972, 522/1973.
Ehituskunst, 5/1991.
F 15 Kontakt, 9/1982
Form Function Finland, 3/1986, 1/1987, 4/1990, 4/1995, 12/1965, 7-8
Numéro special: Formes Finlandaises.
GA document, 11/1984.
GI, 7/1974.
L'Industria delle costruzioni, 186/1987, 218/1989.
Interior Design, 1/1990.
Japan interior design, 224/1977.
Kaavoitus ja rakentaminen, 3/1991.
Kokusai-Kentiku, 2/1967.
Korean Architects, 173/1999.
Kunst und Kirche, 2/1989, 1/1991.
Maison Française, 265/1973.
MD, 4/1981.
Me rakentajat, 3/1996.
Modern Living, 40/1985, 95/1994.
Mur, 3/1983, 1/1985.
Parametro, 106/1982.
Pientalo, 5/1966.
Process: architecture, 37/1983.
Profil, 12/1975.
Progressive Architecture, 2/1986, 2/1989.
Projekt, 3/1978.
Projektiuutiset, 1/1989, 1/1990, 1A/1992, 1/1996, 1/1997, 4/1995, 5/1995, 5/1996, 4/1997, 4/1998.
Puu, 2/1994.

Quaderns, 200/1993.
Rakennustaito, 12/1980, 17/1983, 5/1984, 1/1985, 3/1995, 5/1997.
Rakennusteollisuus, 1/1992, 3/1992.
RSA Journal, 5463/1995.
Spazio e società, 70/1995.
Sportstättenbau + Bäderanlagen, 3/1981.
Takstooli, 2/1991.
Techniques & Architecture, 321/1978, 356/1984, 379/1988.
Teräsrakenne, 4/1984, 3/1991, 3/1992, 1/1998, 2/1998.
Tiili, 4/1979, 1/1980, 2/1980, 4/1983, 3/1984, 3/1987, 1-2/1992.
Toshi-Jutaku, 9/1983.
VilleGiardini, 136/1979.
Werk, Bauen und Wohnen, 10/1974, 12/1975, 10/1980, 6/1983, 4/1987, 4/1988.

Photographic credits

Sebastiano Brandolini
Patrick Degommier
Harri Eronen
Yukio Futagawa
Reto Halme
Daniel Hertzell
Matti Karjanoja
Voitto Niemelä
Max Plunger
Simo Rista
Seppo Saves
Jussi Tiainen
Rauno Träskelin